THE FIGHTING MARLOWS

THE FIGHTING MARLOWS

Men Who Wouldn't Be Lynched

Glenn Shirley

Number Twelve: The Chisholm Trail Series

Texas Christian University Press
Fort Worth

Library of Congress Cataloging-in-Publication Data

Shirley, Glenn.
The fighting Marlows : men who wouldn't be lynched / by Glenn
Shirley.
    p. cm. — (The Chisolm Trail series : no. 12)
    ISBN 0-87565-130-5
    1. Lynching — Texas — Young County — History — 19th century.
    2. Murder — Texas — Young County — History — 19th century. 3.
Marlow family — Trials, litigation, etc. 4. Trials (Murder) — Texas —
Young County. I. Title. II. Series.
    HV6465.T4S53 1994
    364.1'34 — dc20   94-6503
    CIP

Photos of the Marlow family are reproductions of those shown the
author by various Marlow descendants. The poster and scene from *The Sons
of Katie Elder* are from the author's extensive collection of movie memora-
bilia.

Jacket and text design by Barbara Whitehead

Contents

Preface

Many people in northern Texas and southwestern Oklahoma still believe that the Marlow brothers — George, Charles, Alfred (Alf), Lewellyn (Epp), and Boone, the youngest — were thieves and killers. Such opinions, however, are based on legend and folklore. A number of people with family reasons for being interested in the Marlow saga, either circumventing the facts or perhaps never knowing them, have fixed ideas about certain involvements and what did or did not occur.

George and Charles, the only two of the five brothers who survived their complex troubles with the law in Texas and Indian Territory in the 1880s and 1890s, told their side of the controversy in a slim and now exceedingly rare volume entitled *Life of the Marlows, A True Story of Frontier Life in the Early Days. As Related by Themselves* (Plaindealer Print: Kelly & Hulaniski, Publishers, Ouray, Colorado, 1892). This opus, under the same title, revised and edited by William Rathmell and updating the lives of the authors to 1928, was reissued in 100 pages by Ouray Herald Print: W. S. Olexa, Publisher, Ouray, Colorado, and is also quite scarce.

In 1927, Charles A. Siringo gave a somewhat unreliable account of the brothers in *Riata and Spurs, The Story of a Lifetime Spent in the Saddle as Cowboy and Ranger.* Novelisthistorian William MacLeod Raine interviewed George Marlow in Colorado and wrote a more trustworthy resume of the brothers' exploits for *Frontier Stories* magazine (January 1928) entitled "Texas as Was," which was reprinted in his book *Famous Sheriffs and Western Outlaws* (1929). Raine and co-author Will C. Barnes gave them short shrift in *Cattle* (1930). All of this stirred my interest in the Marlow saga and resulted in "Hell Riders of the Brazos" (*Western Aces*, April 1943), which was reprinted as "Buckshot on the Brazos" in my first book, *Toughest of Them All* (1953).

Meanwhile, Texas historian C.L. Sonnichsen included a brief description of the Marlow experience, based on contemporary newspaper accounts, in his book *I'll Die Before I'll Run, The Story of the Great Feuds of Texas* (1951). A second article by Raine, "The Fighting Marlows," appeared in *Empire Magazine* (the *Denver Post*) June 21, 1953, and numerous articles, for the most part heavily fictionalized, have appeared in various western and men's adventure magazines since.

In 1965, Hollywood writer Talbot Jennings saw in the Marlows a powerful tale of primitive struggle, which scriptwriter William H. Wright whipped into a tough, unpretentious and gory little screenplay produced by Hal Wallis for Paramount Pictures, called *The Sons of Katie Elder*. The motion picture was filmed principally in the Pancho Villa country around Durango, Mexico; it was directed by Henry Hathaway, who knew how to spike menace and mayhem with authentic settings and excellent color, and co-starred John Wayne, the screen's foremost western hero, along with Dean Martin.

The story — mostly fiction according to Hollywood standards — deals with a fraternal quartet of prodigals who return to Clearwater, Texas, from their wanderings to confront a hostile community that countenanced the murder of their father years before and swindled their sainted, recently buried mother. The Marlow names are changed to Elder — John (John Wayne), Tom (Dean Martin), Matt (Earl Holliman), and Bud (Michael Anderson, Jr.). The Elders, wrongfully accused of murdering the local sheriff and stealing a herd of horses, are finally captured and fastened two and two together with leg-irons and chains. Highlight of the movie is an attempt to slaughter the brothers in an ambush, from which John and Tom Elder escape with a badly wounded Bud after John severs himself from dead brother Matt by shooting apart their leg chain with a Winchester rifle. The brothers return to town and say they will surrender only to the United States marshal at Laredo. In the climax, John engages his father's murderer in a gun duel and kills him in a fiery conflagration of the latter's store. The Elder name is restored to respectability.

My interest in the Marlows never waned, but I wondered if their real story, pro and con, would ever become known. Then, I was able to locate the records of the United States circuit and district courts for the Northern District of Texas, where the brothers suffered and were charged for their alleged transgressions. From seventeen boxes of papers transferred with the Graham, Young County, federal court to Abilene in 1896 were culled a stack of pleadings and transcripts of testimony which became the primary source for *The Fighting Marlows: Men Who Wouldn't By Lynched.*

The exploits of the Marlow brothers, without this documentation, would seem superhuman. Their fight against mob justice is unparalleled, as lurid a story of love, hate, anger, fear and sudden death as ever sparked the annals of the West.

Glenn Shirley
Stillwater, Oklahoma
1994

I

A Family of Wanderers

The Marlows, by choice and circumstance, were a family of wanderers.[1]

Williamson Marlow, sire of the clan, was born in Tennessee in 1804. Nothing is known of his antecedents and little of his boyhood, except that he was handsome and ever good-natured. When scarcely eighteen, he lived with his child-bride in Nashville, in happiness and comparative prosperity. In 1823, when their first child was born, they joined a brother and sister in southeastern Missouri. During the next few years, the youthful couple were blessed by three other children. The birth of the fourth child resulted in the death of the mother, and life lost its charm for Williamson Marlow.

Leaving his brood in care of the brother and sister, the grief-stricken widower wandered up the Mississippi into Pike County. When the keen edge of his sorrow had worn away, he

1

took up the study of human ills and their cures, and became Dr. Marlow.

Two years later, he crossed the hills and prairies to Jefferson City, thence up the great Missouri to Cooper County. Here he became acquainted with another widower, sturdy John Keton, and his pretty teen-aged daughter Martha, direct descendants of the famous frontiersman, Daniel Boone. Martha's sweet smile and winning ways prolonged the stay of the once gay, now grave and dignified doctor. He set up practice in Cooper County and took Martha Keton for his wife.

Several peaceful years passed during which Martha mothered the doctor's four children and bore him two daughters of her own. In 1849, the doctor was attracted by the gold excitement in California and, like scores of fellow Missourians who left their families, he left his six youngsters in Martha's care and made his way to the land of shining treasure. As the mad rush continued, many men failed and returned to Missouri, broken physically and financially. Others returned with bright hopes and well-filled purses. Among the latter was Dr. Marlow.

The doctor arrived home in time to attend the wedding of his oldest child, a daughter. Shortly afterwards, his first son, James Robert, imbued with tales of the gold rush, departed to view the wonders of the Pacific. The rest of the family moved to Sherman, Texas, an important settlement on the watershed between Red River and the Trinity. Many business houses had moved there from nearby Preston after Grayson County was organized and Sherman established as county seat in 1846. The Marlows lived in a log cabin on the present site of one of the city's finest business blocks.

Memories of old Missouri remained bright in Martha's mind, and the doctor soon moved his practice back to Cooper County. Here Williamson Marlow, Jr. (nicknamed "Willie"), was born in 1853. Two other sons arrived to grace the household — George, on August 11, 1855, and Charles, on November 10, 1860. Then came Alfred (called "Alf") and

Lewellyn (called "Elly" by his mother and later known as "Epp").

These years of domestic tranquility were shattered by the Civil War. P. M. and Bithel Marlow, the doctor's sons by his first wife, became separated. Bithel married a Boonville, Missouri, lass and went to Grayson County, Texas. P. M., serving with the Confederacy, was captured and sent to a northern prison. The remaining Marlows joined a train of 100 wagons and crossed the plains of Kansas to the silver mountains of Colorado. In 1865, they were living near Denver, where Martha's two daughters, Nannie and Charlotte, married two brothers, John and William Murphy. The weddings took place the same day, amid the ringing of bells, feasting and much enjoyment.

In 1866, Dr. Marlow took his family back to Missouri. He found only destruction, the state overrun by ex-guerrillas and scavengers. P. M., released from prison, had gone to Texas and married the daughter of J. W. Whiteaker, a wealthy planter from Austin. Dr. Marlow decided to join his sons in Texas. On the way, the family stopped briefly at Carthage, Missouri. Here, on October 14, Boone Marlow was born, named for Daniel Boone, his famed antecedent.

P. M. and Bithel came to Carthage to visit their father and celebrate the birth of Boone. When they returned to Texas, Dr. Marlow and Willie accompanied them to renew acquaintances at Sherman and survey the country around Austin. Dr. Marlow and Willie then purchased a small herd of cattle and joined a drive up the Chisholm Trail. They sold the herd for a good profit, returned to Carthage, bought mules, wagons and provisions for the entire family and proceeded to Grayson County.

This time the Marlows located between Sherman and Whitesboro, where they put in one hundred acres of crops for a man named Crenshaw. In the early 1870s both P. M. and Bithel died and were buried near their Texas homes. Elizabeth, the fourth and only single Marlow daughter, married a Gainesville gentleman named Gilmore and took a claim below Red River in Wilbarger County. Dr. Marlow took the rest of the family to the western border of the Chickasaw Nation, Indian Territory, to a place he had spotted off the Chisholm Trail, and settled down to farm and practice his profession among the Indians.

The family's home lay in the high rolling hills between Hell Roaring Creek and Rush Creek. The source of Rush Creek was a large spring of pure, wholesome water which flowed at the rate of nearly 300 gallons per minute out of the base of the red sandstone formation underlying the whole region. Rush Creek rose about three miles to the northwest and flowed southeasterly to the Washita River. Numerous small springs on either side of its course made it the most beautiful stream in that part of the Chickasaw Nation.

The spring was a stopping place on the freight trail that carried government supplies from eastern Indian Territory stations for the maintenance of Fort Sill, the soldiers at the fort, and the Indian agency located there. Canvas-topped buckboards drawn by mule teams regularly hauled mail and passengers over the route. A combination slab-and-log inn, store and post office had been constructed on the rise just west of the spring to accommodate freighters and travelers. There was a settlement of six or eight shanties called Rush Springs, and the cabin of Perry Hall, a part Choctaw, who cultivated patches of corn and melons and raised a few sheep. Indians farmed all along the creek. To the southeast lay the range camps of several Texas cattlemen who pastured their herds above the Red River under lease agreements with Chickasaws.

The Marlow boys found occasional work with these outfits — learned to handle longhorns, break broncs and throw the lasso. They fished, trapped and hunted on Hell Roaring Creek and the Washita, so there was always meat in the family larder.

It was a wild, raw country. By treaty of 1855 between the Chickasaws, Choctaws and the United States government, the Chickasaws were given their own nation. Both tribes leased

Above, Dr. Williamson Marlow, father of the Marlow brothers; at right, their mother Martha Marlow.

5

their land west of the 98th meridian on to the government which planned to move the Plains Indians there. This land was called the "Leased District." In 1858, the 98th meridian, forming the western boundary of the Chickasaw Nation, was surveyed, and the Kiowas and Comanches were given a reservation in the southern portion of the district. Later that year the Apaches were settled in the same territory. In 1872, the Wichitas and Caddos were moved to the northeastern portion between the Washita and Canadian rivers, with an agency at Anadarko. They were bordered on the north and west by the Cheyennes and Arapahos. The warring Kiowa, Cheyenne and Comanche who jumped their reservations and set the Texas Panhandle aflame in 1874 had been subjugated, but small bands of hostiles still terrorized the scattered inhabitants on the Chickasaw border. The Chickasaws were under tribal law, and the Leased District was largely policed by troops at Fort Sill. White men were under the jurisdiction of the United States Court for the Western District of Arkansas, at Fort Smith. However, deputy U.S. marshals seldom rode this far west. White desperadoes roamed at will, and private disputes usually were settled with six-shooters.

One morning while some of the Marlow boys were plowing corn, a pistol shot rang out close by, followed by four more shots in quick succession. They ran toward the spot where tiny puffs of smoke rose lazily in the air. There had been a misunderstanding between two neighboring farmers. One man lay wallowing in his blood; the other strolled unconcernedly away. The boys rushed the wounded man to their cabin, where Dr. Marlow's skill as a surgeon saved his life. No arrests were ever made.

The Marlow boys saved enough money to invest in a small herd of Chickasaw cattle, which they drove to a pasture near the Anadarko agency. There was always a ready market for cattle at the agency, but the troops at Fort Sill provided little protection. Once, about fifty Indians swooped down on the boys, yelling, brandishing guns and tomahawks, and scattered the herd in every direction. By pouring showers of Winchester lead into the whooping hostiles who circled them, the brothers escaped to camp with only a few flesh wounds.

After a year of this uncertain existence, the Marlows drove 450 head of horses and cattle north across the Cimarron to a place called Blue Grove, where tall blue joint grass grew rank in the draws and valleys. Here a serious misfortune overtook them. A raging prairie fire swept down on their camp, destroying sixty head of cattle, hundreds of tons of hay, and most of their personal possessions.

Homeless again, they drifted to the Kansas border but found no satisfactory place in that desolate region to reestablish themselves. They disposed of their remaining cattle and horses, purchased mules and wagons, and went back to Texas.

News had spread of the wonderfully fertile soil and abundant riches in Mexico and the Central American countries. Due to the backwardness of the people, their ministers of development sought to attract Europeans pouring across the Atlantic to the United States and Canada by listing potential areas of colonization, theorizing that worthy, hard-working foreigners would improve both the economy and the population. In the spring of 1877, Dr. Marlow, his wife and six sons joined thirty others in a wagon train bound for the balmy climes and flowery lands of the tropics.

At Corpus Christi, they learned that troublesome times in Mexico precluded continuing their journey overland, so all outfits were sold and a brig chartered to take them across the stormy Gulf of Tuxpan. After clearing custom officials and the American consul, the group was separated into families and moved several miles up the Tuxpan River in small boats, rowed by natives, into a veritable Garden of Eden.

For seven months the Marlows grew the finest fruits and vegetables they had ever dreamed of — and prospered. But then Willie contracted malaria. This illness and family restlessness resulted in a decision to return to Texas. Not relishing the rough weather and dangers of the sea they had previously experienced,

7

they went to Tampico to purchase teams and wagons. The only means of conveyance around Tuxpan had been carts, wheelbarrows and pack mules on the mountain trails.

The Marlows found nothing resembling a wagon in Tampico. The American consul was unable to procure a guide across the country. The Mexican minister advised against overland travel without a guard of soldiers, which he declined to furnish. So they abandoned the idea and with little else beyond wearing apparel, took passage on a steamer bound for New Orleans. The journey proved safe and pleasant. From New Orleans, they continued by paddle-wheel boat up the Mississippi and Red rivers to Shreveport, then by wagon to their old grounds in the Lone Star State.

Willie failed to improve. After a brief visit with the Gilmores, the family set out for the mountain air of Leadville, Colorado. They paused among the soldiers at Sheridan's Roost to rest and give Willie a change to recuperate. But Willie was a frail little fellow: his condition worsened in the high altitude, and he was laid to rest in the foothills where bright columbines blossomed and the pine trees sung a requiem.

Leadville, in 1879, equalled Denver in population. Following the new silver strike in the winter of 1876 and 1877, thousands had flocked to the region in quest of fortunes. Miners, demanding higher wages and better working conditions, were on the verge of a strike.

This was not to the Marlows' liking. They heard of the demand for graders, teamsters and tracklayers on the Atchison, Topeka and Santa Fe Railroad building through New Mexico and went south to Las Vegas. Here they hauled ties, then worked on grading crews until Albuquerque became the new terminal and building was started to San Marcial. By the spring of 1880, however, the family was back on the border of the Chickasaw Nation.

They found the Chickasaw country as wild as ever, but more settled than when they had last seen it. Longhorn herds still plodded up the Chisholm Trail to Kansas, but now, after crossing the Cimarron in the Cherokee Outlet, they often turned upriver to intersect the Western or Texas Trail. The Western Trail snaked from Doan's Crossing on the Red River 300 miles northwestward through the Cheyenne-Arapaho reservation and the Outlet to Dodge City. The Chisholm Trail crossed Rush Creek a few miles southeast of Rush Springs, making the springs a favorite camping and watering place for drovers and their herds.

The Marlows settled some seven miles south of Rush Springs, where the trail entered the sand hills above the headwaters of Wild Horse Creek, and built a dugout home called "Marlow Camp." Ten years later, the Chicago, Rock Island and Pacific Railroad would locate its line almost on the trail and establish a station at this point, which was called Marlow.

Though farming for the most part, the family again accumulated a number of cattle. It has been alleged that the brothers fattened their herd from the brands of Texas cattle barons in the Chickasaw Nation and the Kiowa-Comanche-Apache reservation; that it was their nocturnal custom to drive longhorns off the Chisholm Trail to the timber twelve or fifteen miles east of their camp, then return the cattle in a day or two, pretending to have found them straying or in the possession of thieves, and collect rewards; that some of the cattlemen, victimized too often, set a trap and wiped out the band. Of course, no Marlow was killed in such a fight.

Some insight into the Marlows' second sojourn to the Chickasaw border is provided by Harry H. Halsell in his book, *Cowboys and Cattleland*. Harry, his brother Oscar D., and uncle Glenn Halsell ranched in North Texas and had driven thousands of cattle up the Chisholm Trail. In crossing and recrossing Indian Territory, they, like many other drovers, searched east and west of the trail for new grazing areas. In 1881, they were moving a large herd to 10,000 acres of grass called Cowboy Flat in the elbow of the Cimarron, northeast of present Guthrie, Oklahoma.

The herd stopped for the night on Rush Creek. A cow and

a young calf were missing. In mid-afternoon, the trail boss, Mat Laughlin, and a big rough fellow named Charlie Hardwick, had gone back-trailing to find them. The men reached Marlow Camp about four o'clock.

Mrs. Marlow and "one boy about sixteen" (Boone) were at the camp. "Two boys about twenty and twenty-two" (probably Charles and Alf) had just ridden away. There was "about one hundred and twenty-five head" of cattle near the camp, which Laughlin figured had been "picked up as they were lost on the trail," and he told the woman they wanted to examine them. The woman replied, "There are none of your cattle in our bunch, and you let them alone." The boy grabbed Laughlin's bridle rein. The woman covered him with a pistol. Hardwick drew his six-shooter, told the boy to "turn loose," and the woman to "put away her gun." Both complied.

Laughlin and Hardwick loped to the herd and started checking the brands. Mrs. Marlow "opened on them with a long-range gun." The other two Marlow boys galloped up at the same time, firing Winchesters, and the men "left in a hurry."

Halsell, who also had been hunting the cow and calf, was returning to camp at sundown when Laughlin and Hardwick came riding toward him at full speed. "The Marlows are after us," Laughlin shouted, "and you had better come on." Halsell found the cow and calf later that evening near Hell Roaring Creek.

The outfit camped on Rush Creek until noon the next day. While they were at dinner, "two fine-looking cowboys" rode up, dismounted, went to the chuck wagon and loaded their plates with beans and bread. They sat down and ate "conveniently near their horses," and visited with the trail hands "like they were old acquaintances." After they left, Laughlin and Hardwick told Halsell they were the pair who had shot at them the afternoon before. Halsell described their visit as "one of the coolest and bravest acts I ever saw."[2]

During their stay on Wild Horse Creek, the Marlow broth-

ers often assisted the "heavy barons," as they called Texas cattlemen, in driving their herds through this section of the
Indian Territory. On one occasion, they accompanied a trail
herd to Wichita, Kansas.

George himself worked for a rancher named Ed Walsh in
the northern part of the Kiowa-Comanche-Apache reservation and did odd jobs around Fort Sill. One afternoon when
he had drawn some money due him at the fort and was about
to start home, a young Indian accosted him, and said: "You
steal Indian's pony."

"Indian lies," replied George. "I bought this pony and it is
mine."

But the Indian insisted vehemently and grasped the bridle
reins. George stuck a six-shooter under his nose and informed
him that if he did not disappear at once he would find himself
in the happy hunting grounds.

Four more Indians quickly appeared with their interpreter.
After listening to their gutteral argument for a few moments,
the interpreter told George: "They want you to go to the
commanding officer, and you had better go, as that is the best
way to settle the matter."

George accompanied them to the officer's quarters. The
interpreter explained that, a few days previous, someone had
stolen a horse from the Indians and they recognized it as the
one George was riding. George had purchased the horse from
Ed Walsh and offered to bring in the bill of sale.

"How long have you had the pony?" the officer asked.

"About six months."

"Well, if you let these Indians take your horse, it is your
fault," the officer said.

George thanked him, sprang into the saddle, set spurs to
the pony's flanks, and was out of the fort like a flash. He was
half a mile across the prairie before noticing the Indians in hot
pursuit.

It was five to one if it came to a fight. George rode with the
speed of the wind. His pony showed signs of exhaustion as he

approached camp. His brothers heard his shouts and rode out to meet him. The Indians stopped and turned back, the four Marlows after them.

According to George, "The boys returned late in the evening, tired and thirsty . . . made little comment at all, though they brought back quite a supply of weapons they didn't have when they started."[3]

Excepting this difficulty, the Marlows got along well with the Indians — even participated in some of their tricks.

George recalled: "One time we were helping drive a big herd through the territory and a little band of Indians rode up and asked us for a steer. Said they had no meat and were hungry. My brothers and I had always been kind to the Indians in matters like this, so they came to us. We told them to go to the boss, and likely he would give them a critter. We also gave them some pointers as to how to get a good one. . . .

"They struck the boss for a donation, and he picked out the stubbiest and most runty yearling in the bunch. Charley and I winked at the bucks as they started with their little yearling. As they got toward the middle of the herd, they gave the most curdling yells, and the cattle stampeded in forty directions. There was upwards of a thousand of 'em and in rounding 'em up us boys had no time to look after the Indians.

"Well, those red rascals dropped their runt of a yearling, cut out the fattest and best four-year-old steer they could find, and before we knew it they were two or three miles over the prairie and out of sight."[4]

Things were quiet at Marlow Camp for another year. The Marlow herd increased. George courted a young lady, "prepossessing and of fair accomplishments," named Lillian Berry, who "was born in Kansas near the Nebraska border" and, like the Marlow brothers, had been reared in several different states. She "stole George's heart away," and on June 17, 1883, they were "made man and wife in the Indian Territory, on the Washita."

The following spring, the entire family trekked across the

Cimarron, thence northwestward upriver to Trinidad, Colorado. They sold their cattle in the railroad camps and quit the stock business temporarily. Dr. Marlow, his wife and Charles made a trip overland to California to visit James Robert and revel in the sights where, thirty-five years before, the doctor had mined a stake from the placer diggings.

But the pioneer days of the Golden Gate country had faded forever, replaced by churches, colleges and the market of commercial traffic. This was not to the liking and habits of the Marlows. They soon returned to Trinidad, picked up the rest of the family, and again journeyed to Texas via the Fort Sill country.

The family crossed Red River west of Cache Creek into the Big Wichita Valley and camped northeast of Wichita Falls. Here the years of wandering ended for Dr. Marlow. He died on April 12, 1885, and was laid to rest beneath the grass-covered prairie he had loved so long and well.

The Fort Worth and Denver Railroad had reached Wichita Falls in 1882, booming the little freight line terminus into one of the largest cattle-shipping points in North Texas. It also was a supply center patronized by Indians and soldiers from Fort Sill.

The railroad was building toward Vernon, in Wilbarger County, and the Marlow brothers took a grading contract. At this place, Alf Marlow courted and married Miss Zenia Davis, "a handsome Western lass, brave and true-hearted," who proved entirely worthy as a life companion.[5]

Wilbarger County's northern boundary, the Red River, cornered the Kiowa-Comanche-Apache reservation and the unassigned, Texas-claimed Greer country stretching northwestward along the North Fork of the Red, which was the reservation's western border. Excepting a few settlers like the Marlows' sister Elizabeth Gilmore and her husband living on the uplands between Doan's Crossing and Vernon, the county was covered with ranches. The big ranchers were crusty individualists of the rough-and-tumble school. The lesser stock-

13

men either sought their favor or owed them money and, although less concerned, were strongly influenced by their prejudices against "nesters" and fringe operators, who were viewed as thieves.

The Marlows camped at the Gilmore home until their railway contract was completed. Wishing to stay close to their sister but away from the ranches, they purchased twenty head of horses, crossed into the Greer country, and located in the horseshoe bend of the North Fork of Red River near the Navajo Mountains.

Here seven peaks rise abruptly to a maximum height of a thousand feet above the prairie and extend north and south across the open end of the bend made as the river sweeps eastward, then back in a loop four or five miles in diameter. In the mid-1800s legend has it, a war party of Navajos dropped south of the Santa Fe Trail to prey on the horse herds of the Comanches. A band of Comanche warriors surprised them in camp at the base of the mountains and killed them. One managed to escape and stayed in the mountains for some time. Thus the peaks were named the Navajos.

The Marlows took a claim on the North Fork below the junction of its Elm Fork tributary. While Martha Marlow, George's wife, and Boone cared for the stock, George, Charles and Epp erected corrals and dwellings. Alf and his bride left on a brief wedding tour to visit some of Zenia's relatives. Shortly after their return, Boone crossed the Red River to visit sister Elizabeth.

James Holdson, a cowboy allegedly employed to intimidate settlers, had stopped at the Gilmore home. As Boone approached, he stepped from the doorway and, without a word, drew a revolver and began shooting. With lead whistling close to his ears, Boone dismounted, drew his Winchester from his saddle, and put a bullet through the man's heart.

Elizabeth and her husband rushed from the house, saw

Holdson lying on the ground and Boone standing with a smoking rifle.

"Oh, Boone," Elizabeth cried, running to him. "What have you done?"

"In God's name, Sis," replied Boone, "who is that man and why did he want to kill me?"

Elizabeth did not know. "He came asking questions and was half drunk, too. He must have mistaken you for someone else."

"Well," responded Boone, "it was a bad mistake. What shall we do?"

Gilmore knelt beside the dead man, examined the wound, and said: "I'll notify the sheriff. You were perfectly justified in shooting him, Boone, but there is no telling what trouble may result. You had better seek safety."

Boone galloped home and told his brothers what had happened. They considered the conditions and circumstances and agreed that Gilmore had given him good advice. They thrust some money into Boone's pockets and packed his warbag while he saddled a fresh mount. Then Boone kissed his mother and was off to Colorado.[6]

The Wilbarger County sheriff apparently was satisfied with Elizabeth's and her husband's account of Holdson's death. At least he took no action. Many, however, blamed Boone for his haste and lack of judgment. If it was a case of self-defense, why had he fled?

The matter continued to simmer. Some time previously, Texas Rangers had been called to Wilbarger County to break up a mob, which included the sheriff, organized to hang cattle thieves. The vigilante tendency of local citizens and threats of reprisal by Holdson's friends greatly disturbed Martha Marlow.

Martha Marlow had belonged to the Christian Church for twenty-five years and carried a testament with her wherever the family wandered. Of a Spartan nature, she rejoiced in the stern denunciation of the prophets — a tooth for a tooth, an eye for an eye. Her love for her sons was as their love for her. She asked only that the world let her and hers alone. None of her sons had ever broken the law. Boone had killed to save his life.

Martha felt it best that the family pull stakes before more blood was shed. Driving two covered wagons and riding horseback, they followed Boone to Colorado.

Boone rejoined them at Trinidad, where the family sold their horses and rested. George, meanwhile, visited the Western Slope to survey Gunnison Valley.

Gold had been discovered in the Tin Cup and Washington Gulch districts in 1861, but not until 1879 were reports so favorable as to cause a rush second to none in the history of the state. Mining towns sprang up throughout the valley, with Gunnison City as the supply center and county seat. While the existence of gold was known, the production of lead-silver ores received almost undivided attention, albeit with only a small margin of profit. In 1885 attention turned to prospecting for gold, and the results were highly satisfactory.

The Continental Divide or Saguache Range formed the east line of Gunnison County, in a general north-south direction. Its main drainage was the Gunnison River, formed by the junction of the Slate and Taylor rivers nine miles north of Gunnison City and flowing westward from the county south of its center through the great Black Cañon. Numerous tributaries joined the river in Black Cañon — the principle streams being Curecanti, Sapinero, West Elk and Ohio creeks, from the north, and Lake Fork and White Earth creeks, from the south. The Tomichi River, which joined the Gunnison near Gunnison City, carried the waters from the southeast. The North Fork of the Gunnison carried the drainage from the northwest.

George Marlow became enamored with the beauty of the valley and saw an opportunity more lasting than the quest for gold and silver — raising small fruits and vegetables to supply the mining camps. For ages the disintegration of the mountains had poured unlimited tons of sediment into the valley, building a silt and rich loam impregnated with nitrates, potash and other elements which would produce record crops with the wonderful system of natural drainage and proper irrigation. George envisioned a Garden of Eden greater than his father had found in Mexico.

Cyrus Wells "Doc" Shores, the sheriff of Gunnison County, shared George's enthusiasm and lent encouragement. Shores, like George Marlow, was a typical cowboy, ready to ride a wild bronc, lasso a steer, or run a foot race. As a lad, he had come west from Michigan and up the Missouri on a steamer to Fort Benton, where he became a bullwhacker. He had freighted from Montana to Texas, driven longhorns to the Kansas railheads, and arrived in Gunnison City with his wife and two freight wagons in 1880. The woeful lack of law enforcement in the valley caused him to seek the office of sheriff in 1884. He was widely acclaimed for apprehending bank and train bandits and stock thieves, and bringing toughs under control — usually without parading his authority or displaying a gun. He also served the section as a deputy United States marshal.

Shortly after George's arrival at Gunnison City, he and Sheriff Shores became fast friends: "We passed the time pleasantly, and neither of us could have been made to believe that, at a not far distant day, we would be tangled in a transaction that would lack almost nothing of terminating the life of one of us. . . ."[7]

George hied himself back to Trinidad. But Martha Marlow, remembering the tribulations of the family's Mexico venture, nixed his plan. His brothers had purchased oxen, new wagons and necessities for an overland trip to the strip of public domain between Colorado and Texas, known as No Man's Land.

The strip, 167 miles long and thirty-five miles wide, had been set aside by Congress, in fixing the northern boundary of the Texas Panhandle in 1850, as a "neutral" highway for Mexican traders doing business in Kansas. After U.S. troops ended the Kiowa and Comanche raids on the route in 1864,

Cyrus Wells "Doc" Shores, sheriff of Gunnison County, Colorado.

Colorado and New Mexico sheepmen took advantage of the free grass. Cattlemen soon followed. By 1885, nearly 3,000 settlers had occupied the area and established half a dozen towns, with Beaver, on the Beaver River, as the self-proclaimed capital. All of which Congress ignored. Without legal restraints, courts or land offices, the settlers fared for themselves. No Man's Land would remain outside any state or federal jurisdiction another five years.

Though nothing more had been heard of the Holdson killing in Texas, Martha Marlow remained concerned. She felt that Boone would be safe in the strip. George postponed his Gunnison Valley dream.

All five brothers took claims which they worked to good advantage by hunting and trapping. Prairie chicken and quail were in abundance and in the winter were joined by great flocks of wild ducks and geese. A few buffalo still roamed the rugged hill country to the west and were hard to kill. But it was easy to bring home an antelope or a deer. That winter Charles Marlow also took a wife, a young lady named Emma Copenbarger, whom all happily welcomed into the family circle.

Then came the blizzard of January 1886.

The west wind shifted to the north just before midnight December 31, and a thirty-five mile an hour gale struck the unprotected prairies with fierce gusts of sleet and snow. Temperatures in central and western No Man's Land dropped to twenty degrees below zero. Roads became impassable under six-foot drifts. Snow covered some dugout homes and houses so completely that the chimneys could not draw the smoke from the rooms. Hundreds of townsmen, settlers and cowboys attending New Year's celebrations were stranded for days in hotels and business establishments. Many others, caught far from home and shelterless, froze to death. Thousands of head of livestock perished.

The Marlows were on a hunting trip. They tied all the blankets in camp over the shivering forms of their horses and turned them loose, then dug a pit for themselves and covered

The Marlow brothers at Fort Sill, Indian Territory, about 1887: left to right, George, Boone, Alfred (Alf), Lewellyn (Epp), and Charles.

it with wagon canvas. They kept a roaring fire at one end of the hole, having over 200 pounds of buffalo tallow to feed its flames. When the storm abated, they made their way afoot to their claims over great tracts of land blighted by horror, suffering and death.

Many cattlemen who had worked hard to build up their herds in this "cowman's paradise" grimly stayed on and laid the foundation for the present livestock industry of the region. Others, however, hung up "For Rent" signs and drove what was left of their herds to more inviting climes. Land-hungry "grangers," as the settlers were called, watched with interest this cowman's flight and quickly occupied unclaimed areas. Thus began the transition of the country from ranch to farm.

Much of the strip's wildlife had been destroyed. In the spring, the Marlows moved south again to the familiar environs of the Kiowa-Comanche-Apache reservation. George, Epp and Boone obtained an agency permit to farm some Comanche land near Anadarko. Martha Marlow stayed with them. Charles and Alf, with their wives, went to work near Fort Sill for an Indian named Sunday Boy.

At this stage of their wandering, clannish existence, the five brothers looked to be ordinary men — wiry, tanned, weather-beaten, with brown or blue eyes and light brown or blond hair. George and Charles wore drooping mustaches. Boone was the smallest; he stood five feet seven inches in high-heeled boots, weighed 145 pounds, wore a light, thin mustache, and was slightly bowlegged. Epp and Alf were the strongest — Alf a brute of a man. All were slow-talking and mild-mannered but ready to fight for each other should the need arise. That need was at hand. They were soon to write a bloody chapter in the history of Young County, Texas.

21

II

Young County — No Stranger to Violence

Young County was no stranger to violence. It was created on February 2, 1856, organized the same year, and named for Colonel William C. Young, a Tennessee lawyer who had come to Texas in 1837, served as first sheriff of Red River County, district attorney of the Seventh Judicial District of the Republic of Texas, and soldier in the Mexican War. At the outbreak of the Civil War, he organized and commanded the 11th Texas Regiment of Confederate cavalry, made up from eleven Texas counties. In May 1861, he crossed the Red River, capturing Forts Arbuckle, Washita and Cobb in Indian Territory. Shortly afterwards, in poor health, he returned to his home — then in Cooke County — where he was instrumental in exposing a plot by Union sympathizers to resist the Confederate draft and spy for the Union army. Sixty some men were taken into custody in Cooke and adjoining counties and placed under guard at Gainesville, where thirty-nine were convicted by a "citizen's court" for conspiracy and insurrection or disloyalty and treason and hanged on October 1, 1862. About two weeks later, the ailing Colonel Young was assassinated in the canebrakes on Red River.[1]

The Marlows knew nothing of Young. But while farming near Whitesboro, they had heard much about the Great Hanging, still fresh in the minds and hearts of Texans in 1868.

The Brazos River crossed the west and south portions of Travis County. Within county boundaries lay the Brazos Indian Reservation and Fort Belknap, a United States army post established in 1851 by General William G. Belknap to maintain peace on the frontier. The military post's environs became a stopping place for mail and passenger stages on the Butterfield Overland Mail route from Dallas, as well as for freighters supplying the fort and reservation. The area's population increased to over 500, and the town of Belknap was designated the county seat when Young County was organized in 1856.

The first county court was held in August 1856, with Peter Harmonson presiding. Harmonson also acted as county treasurer and carried the treasury in his belt at no risk, the entire collection from taxes the first year being less then $200. Court sessions were held in government buildings until a thirty-by-eighteen-foot concrete structure was erected for a clerk's office and courthouse in February 1857. A small log jail was completed in September, but bail was usually given due to the difficulty of holding prisoners. Many released prisoners never returned before the bar of justice.

The first state district court was held in November 1858, Judge Nathaniel M. Burford of Dallas presiding. The grand jury found sixty-five indictments ranging from murder and assault to murder to altering cattle brands and gambling. In September 1859, Major Robert S. Neighbors, supervising

24

agent for the Texas Indians, was slain at Belknap by one Edward Cornett, who resented Neighbor's comments about the recent killing of an Indian by white men. Cornett was never tried for his crime. He was found dead a few months later in the Belknap Hills.

Fees for county officials were minimal, and Young County was served by half a dozen judges and seven sheriffs before and during the Civil War. H. S. Cox, elected sheriff in 1864, was killed by Indians soon after he took office. No other sheriff was elected, since the county was in the throes of reorganization.

When Texas seceded from the Union, Fort Belknap was practically abandoned and the residents of Belknap sought more thickly populated areas. It was no longer a safe place even for county records, and in May 1865, these were transferred to the care of adjoining Jack County. The fort was reoccupied after the war and maintained a few years for the protection of settlers and travelers. The town's population had been reduced to 135 residents plus four slaves. When Young County was reorganized in 1874, the seat was moved to Graham on the Salt Creek tributary of the Brazos. Belknap lost its post office and most of its remaining citizens.

Graham was founded in 1872 by Gustavus A. and Edwin S. Graham of the Graham Brothers Salt Works, operated on Salt Creek before the war. Other businesses were the Cloud and McDonald Milling Company, which included a gristmill, sawmill and gin; a brick kiln; the Commerce and Graham hotels; the weekly *Graham Leader*, edited by forty-six-year-old Indiana-born newspaperman Joseph W. Graves; various retail stores; a livery stable; blacksmith and saddle shops; and the usual thirst emporiums.

The principal occupations were farming and stock raising. Most farmers also ran cattle. Old brand books list preachers, lawyers, doctors and other professionals as having a few head of beef and a horse or two. Stock theft was common on the ranges of Young and adjoining counties and was the incentive for organizing the Cattle Raisers' Association of Texas at Graham in

1877. More than one-tenth of the county's 4,500 citizens located in Graham as the new county seat grew rapidly.

Though county revenues remained small, a full compliment of officials was elected in 1874. The first term of state district court in Graham was held in November 1875, Judge A. J. Hood of Weatherford, Parker County, presiding. Vacant rooms and little frame buildings were used for grand and petit juries until a courthouse and a jail were erected.

This general harmony was interrupted by more bloodshed.

In February 1876, Sheriff Richard Kirk went to Belknap to arrest a desperado called Buffalo Bill, who had shot and seriously wounded Colonel W. S. Ikard, a prominent drover in Clay County. Buffalo had escaped from the Clay County jail. He recognized Sheriff Kirk as the officer approached. Both men drew their guns simultaneously, and when the smoke cleared both lay in the street, dead.

Graham's real surge of growth began in November 1877 when the Texas delegation in Congress drafted a bill to create a new federal judicial district and rearrange the existing districts of the state. This bill placed the courts at Galveston, Tyler, and Jefferson in the Eastern District of Texas, and Brownsville, San Antonio, and Austin in the Western District. In April 1879, three federal courts were created in the Northern District at Graham, Waco and Dallas. The jurisdiction of the Graham court extended over seventy-two northwestern counties from the Santa Fe railroad through Gainesville on the east, the Texas and Pacific through Abilene on the south, and west to the Territory of New Mexico. Andrew Phelps McCormick was made judge of the Graham division.

McCormick was forty-seven, a native of Brazoria County and the son of Scottish immigrants from Ireland. He graduated with honors from Danville (Kentucky) College in 1854, was admitted to the Texas bar in 1855, and practiced in Brazoria until he joined the Confederate army in 1861. After the war, he was district judge at Brazoria, a delegate to the constitutional conventions of 1866 and 1869, and judge of the 18th Judicial District of Texas from 1871 until elected Republican senator to the state legislature in 1876. He was a United States attorney for the Eastern District of Texas when appointed to the Graham division of the Northern District.

The judge moved his wife and six children to Graham after the court was officially designated and located in June 1879. So impressed were the citizens with his presence that they gave him a southern antebellum-style home at 710 Cherry Street, which still stands as one of the best examples of the town's architectural beauty. On August 4, he opened the first federal court in the upper story of the then-imposing stone building just constructed by druggist Joseph E. Ryus at 608 Oak Street. Graham became one of the most important and liveliest places in North Texas.

As if McCormick had not enough responsibility, by act of Congress on January 6, 1883, all that portion of Indian Territory lying west of the Chickasaw Nation between the South Canadian and Red rivers (which included the Fort Sill country) was taken from the jurisdiction of the Western District of Arkansas and annexed to the Northern District of Texas. From that date Judge McCormick's docket was a full one. People from the many counties in the Graham division and elsewhere taxed the capacity of the town's facilities during court terms. Indians camped on the Salt Creek and added much color to the sessions. They spent their witness money freely, and the *Graham Leader* frequently complained of having to explain the redman's signs and hieroglyphics.

By 1877, the United States commissioner at Graham was Francis W. Girand, a Kentucky-born cousin of Judge McCormick's and a major in Hood's Brigade during the Civil War. William Lewis "Old Tige" Cabell, a brigadier-general in the Trans-Mississippi Department during the war, was United States marshal at Dallas, and Charles B. Pearre was United States attorney. Representing Marshal Cabell in the Graham division during the 1880s was a thirty-four-year-old deputy marshal named Edward W. "Ed" Johnson.

27

Johnson was a native of Clark County, Arkansas, where he had served as deputy sheriff before coming to Texas in 1880. He was a deputy in Clay County when commissioned by Cabell in 1885. He was a large, square-jawed man who had lost his right arm in a battle with one Bob James at Wichita Falls in February of 1888. But he could still handle a revolver with his left hand, having practiced a great deal, and was an effective officer.

On the local level rode Sheriff Marion D. Wallace and County Attorney P. A. Martin, a native of Wilks County, North Carolina — elected to office in 1884 and 1886, respectively. Martin was assisted by Robert "Bob" Holman, a local attorney, who hailed from the Blue Grass regions of Kentucky.

No one in Young County at this time knew that "P. A." — as Martin was affectionately called — was the same Phelete A. Martin who had been convicted of the felonious slaying of William B. Reeves in Superior Court of Iredell County, North Carolina, before coming to Texas in 1882 and taking up the practice of law. He was considered a prudent prosecutor. Many Young County badmen had found refuge in the Indian reservations, and Martin often accompanied Deputy Johnson on posse trips in the discharge of his duties, but more for pleasure than anything else and because he wanted to see the country.

Nor was much known of Sheriff Wallace's early life. He and his wife, descended from some of the most noted families of Alabama, farmed between Graham and Belknap. "Little Marion" A. Wallace, the sheriff's nephew, lived with them. The *Graham Leader* considered the Wallaces "fine people"; that "those who have been blessed with our sheriff's acquaintance" could say "there lives no braver, gentler, kindlier man than he. . . . To friends he is all generosity; to strangers . . . all hospitality, to those in trouble . . . a friend; to those who sorrow . . . ever faithful; and to those who violate the laws of the state . . . a mortal terror."[2]

McCormick, Girand, Cabell, Johnson, Martin, Holman and Wallace soon became familiar names in the Marlow lexicon.

III

Charged With Horse Thievery
and Murder

It is difficult to understand
how, down the years, the Marlows have been classed as thieves
and killers-in-hiding. No evidence exists that the small herds
they accumulated and sold for profit were stolen. They were
generally considered innocent of evildoing, Boone excepted,
and the Holdson affair apparently had been forgotten as the
brothers continued to work in the Fort Sill country throughout 1887. Lillian Marlow bore George a daughter, Myrtle. In
the spring of 1888, George left Lillian and the child with
Charles' and Alf's wives to take another look at Gunnison
Valley, where he renewed his acquaintance with Sheriff
Shores, put up hay and dug ditches on an irrigation project.
The Marlows were hiding from nobody.

It was primarily an odious practice of U. S. commissioners
that brought on the Marlow troubles. The comissioners

29

would issue blank warrants, which deputy marshals served at their own discretion wherever a suspect could be found. Often a deputy had no warrant and only flimsy evidence. He received no fixed salary and depended on the government's pecuniary compensation of six cents a mile when on official business and two dollars for an arrest. The fee system resulted in impositions to such an extent that the best citizens came to look upon some marshals as a greater curse than the thieves and killers they pursued.[1]

Toward the end of August 1888, Deputy Marshal Ed Johnson allegedly received a telegram from one "Doc Burns," sheriff of Las Animas County, Colorado, asking him to be on the lookout for "the five Marlow brothers," who were "endeavoring to get away with forty head of horses," stolen at Trinidad. While en route to Indian Territory, Johnson allegedly received a second message from Burns, stating that "the parties owning [the horses] have since found them. They had only strayed." Instead of explaining the situation to his posse and returning to Graham, Johnson thrust the message into his pocket and continued on his mission to arrest Boone, Epp, Alf and Charles Marlow.[2]

Strangely, neither message was ever produced to a federal grand jury or in U. S. commissioners or the Graham district court. There is no evidence that such communications existed. In addition, the Marlows had not been in Trinidad since leaving for No Man's Land nearly two years earlier. Finally, William T. Burns was sheriff of Las Animas County, Colorado, in 1888. He was an early day stockgrower and never known as "Doc." Early writers possibly confused Burns with Sheriff Shores of Gunnison.

Deputy Johnson did go to Indian Territory in August — not at the request of any Colorado sheriff but to investigate the theft of a number of Indian ponies. He was accompanied by Dink Allen and Sam Criswell, trusted allies who had been with him on many expeditions into the reservations. Johnson had never seen the Marlows but, learning that they traded with the Indians and owned a number of horses, he connected them with the thievery for some reason never explained satisfactorily.

Popular assumption was that his action stemmed from the rustling that plagued Texas ranchers who had pastures in the Fort Sill country. Big rewards had been offered, but few of the thieves were apprehended, and the ranchers had long pressured Johnson for relief. The Cattle Raisers' Association wielded great political influence, and the twin inducements — rewards plus the security of his post — overrode any scruples. The deputy apparently felt that he must make a showing and chose the Marlows.[3]

George Marlow maintained: "The rich cattle barons practically ruled the country. . . . Johnson had made little headway against these rustlers, so he determined to arrest somebody, fearing the stockmen would lose confidence in his ability and knowing full well that in that frontier region it was easier to convict an innocent man of horse-stealing than a guilty man of murder." Because of the nomadic life of the brothers, Johnson "thought it would be an easy matter to swear them into the penitentiary" and collect his fees.[4]

Speculation aside, court records of the Northern District of Texas show that, on August 8, 1888, Johnson appeared before U.S. Commissioner Girand and declared "upon reasonable and credible information" that Alf, Charles, Epp and Boone Marlow, "on March 1855 . . . did unlawfully and feloniously take, steal, carry away and dispose of 19 head of horses from a Caddo Indian named Ba-Sinda-Bar." A warrant for Alf, Charles, Epp and Boone was issued accordingly.[5]

Johnson and posse — which now included J. C. Carson, chief of the Anadarko agency police — reached the place where Boone, Epp and their mother were living, on Saturday, August 25. Martha Marlow was alone. She knew none of the riders, nor did they identify themselves as officers. It was a warm afternoon, and she cordially invited them into the house, out of the sun. They declined, asking for water, and she drew a fresh bucket from the well.

Johnson pretended to be gathering men to drive some cattle and wanted to hire her boys. Were they around?

The unsuspecting mother told him that George was on his way home from Colorado; Charles and Alf were digging potatoes for Sunday Boy near Fort Sill; Boone and a lad named Metz were gathering corn in a field nearby; Epp had gone over to a neighbor's, but would be back soon.

Johnson thanked her and departed with his posse, stating that perhaps they would meet Epp on the way, return with him and talk over whatever deal they might make with Boone. Upon meeting Epp, they drew their guns, and shouted: "Hands up!" Epp was so astonished that the order was repeated a third time before he obeyed. The posse then proceeded with their prisoner to the cornfield, arrested Boone and young Metz, and directed them to unload the corn as they needed their team of mules and wagons to convey them to Anadarko.

The prisoners were chained to the wagon, and as the cavalcade approached the house, Martha Marlow rushed toward them, demanding an explanation.

Johnson blocked her path, stating emphatically: "You know what your thieving sons have done. We are taking them to the agency, and you cannot go near them. Do you understand?"

"I have started to my boys," replied Martha Marlow, "and god help me, I shall do so even if it costs my life."

She darted past Johnson with more agility than he thought she possessed and reached the wagon before he could stop her.

The officers shoved her aside and held her at bay while they searched the house for firearms. They found a shotgun and rifle belonging to Boone, and Epp's six-shooter and Winchester. Then the prisoners were driven away. The aged mother followed, plodding as closely behind the wagon as her tiring legs would permit, despite the curses and threats hurled at her.

Within a quarter mile of Anadarko, Johnson took the prisoners from the wagon, deciding for some reason to walk them into the agency. Boone and Epp persuaded their mother to care for the team and wagon, find lodging for the night, and come see them the next morning. Johnson, having made no headway with the woman by his harsh treatment, agreed.

Martha Marlow was at the jail at sunup. She waited a tiresome hour before Johnson appeared. He politely asked her to return home, get her sons a change of clothes, and come back that afternoon when she could visit with them as long as she wished.

At 1:00 P.M. the mother was back at the jail, only to be informed by Chief Carson that Johnson and posse had left with the prisoners in a lumber wagon four hours previously en route to Fort Sill.

In speaking of this betrayal afterwards, Mrs. Marlow said: "Johnson showed so plainly to me what kind of material his being was constructed. When I was told that this man had taken my dear boys away, I felt as though I was choking to death. My heart stood perfectly still for a few moments, then beat so fast I thought it would burst from my bosom."[6]

It was only the beginning of Martha Marlow's disappointment and grief.

Johnson and posse reached Fort Sill with their prisoners late in the afternoon and spent the night. The following morning, they drove twelve miles to Sunday Boy's place, where they surprised Charles and Alf Marlow and took their weapons. When arrested, Charles had a Winchester and a six-shooter; Alf had "a six-shooter, a long-range rifle with a globe sight, and a shotgun his father-in-law had given him."[7]

At Sunday Boy's place, young Metz was released. He had been held only to keep him from informing Charles and Alf of the arrest of Epp and Boone. The wives of Charles and Alf and George's wife and child were sent under guard to Anadarko to join "the poor mother." Charles and Alf were handcuffed and chained in the wagon with Epp and Boone, and the four prisoners started a distance of seventy-five miles to Graham on August 29, 1888.[8]

Johnson and posse arrived in Graham on Tuesday evening, September 4, lodged the Marlows in the county jail (where federal prisoners also were fed and kept), and told the *Graham Leader* that the brothers were "desperate characters" who had been in the "horse business" in Indian Territory "for six years." Further, "they had in possession a goodly number of the best Sharps rifles and if Mr. Johnson had failed to get the drop on them they would no doubt have made it lively for the posse." Johnson claimed that he had seized "an enormous amount of buffalo guns, .45 six-shooters, shotguns and carbine rifles, and plenty of ammunition." Asked what he had done with this arsenal, he replied that it had been "left at Fort Sill."[9]

On September 5, Johnson appeared before U.S. Commissioner Girand and declared "upon reasonable and credible information" that Alf, Charles, Epp and Boone Marlow "did, on about March 1886 . . . unlawfully and feloniously take, steal, carry away and dispose of about 20 head of horses, the property of Black Crow, a Comanche Indian." [10] The same date, Johnson also charged that the four brothers "did, on about January or February 1866 . . . take, steal, carry away and dispose of 13 head of horses, the property of one Washington, a Caddo Indian."[11]

Warrants were issued by Commissioner Girand, which Johnson executed by "arresting [defendants] and delivery in open court at examination before F. W. Girand, U.S. Commissioner . . . and not giving bond required [$500 each] delivered the within defts. in jail at Graham."[12]

Meanwhile, George Marlow found his mother and other womenfolk at Anadarko and learned that Alf, Charles, Epp and Boone had been arrested. In light of the accusation, special Indian agent and inspector E. E. White (serving temporarily as agent for the Kiowas in 1888) had ordered the Marlow women out of the Territory.

George knew nothing of the matter except what his mother told him:"I went to Agent White," he recorded,

> and asked for a permit to camp close to the agency while we gathered our livestock and personal property. He asked my name, I told him, and he said 'Consider yourself under arrest.' I asked 'What for? Where are your papers?' and he said Mr. Johnson had authorized him to hold me; that he would wire Johnson, and if he did not want me, I would be released.
>
> My Indian friends proved how sincere their regard was for me. They helped gather our 31 horses and mares, a colt, and a span of mules — load our wagons, and start our families out of there for Graham. . . . Every nic-nac or sweet that they thought I would eat was brought to me. I do not know if White heard anything from Johnson — I was released after four days. . . . My wife had left me a horse, and I overtook my family on Red River.
>
> After crossing into Texas, we camped on Salt Creek [above Graham]. I came into town, saw Sheriff Wallace and asked if we could see the boys. He said we could, so I went back for mother and the boys' wives . . . went up to the jail about two o'clock in the afternoon, saw the boys, then went east of town with our horses and wagons to an old water tank, and camped. . . .
>
> I went to cutting cord wood for a fellow, and we stayed in that camp over two weeks. I came to town every other day to see the boys and bring them a little nourishing chuck, and secured the services of an attorney — Robert Arnold. He took the boys' case for $500, which I paid without a word. I would have paid three times the amount had it been asked, as I was as ignorant of courts, laws and lawyers as a new born babe. Arnold turned out to be a bosom friend of Johnson's. . . . In a few days, I was arrested.

Sam Criswell came by the camp after dark and I told him to have a chair. He said, 'No — I will have to pull you.' I asked what for and he said, 'That is the orders of Ed.' I asked 'Where are your papers?' He said Ed had them. I said, 'I will come in the morning.' He said, 'No, come in now, Ed is out there.' [Johnson apparently chose to remain outside the camp rather than face the wrath of Martha Marlow].

I went out in the road, found Johnson and asked him for the papers. He said he did not have them with him but would show them to me in town. We came into Graham, and he put me in jail. . . . I never saw any papers at all.[13]

George was arrested the evening of October 6. The next day, Johnson declared before U.S. Commissioner Girand that "George Marlow did, on March 1885 . . . take, steal, carry away and appropriate to his own use 19 head of horses, the property of Ba-Sinda-Bar, a Caddo Indian."[14] This was the same theft claimed by Johnson in his charge against Alf, Charles, Epp and Boone on August 8. Girand promptly issued a warrant, which Johnson executed by "delivering [defendant] in open court . . . and placing him in jail [in lieu of bail] under this writ."[15]

At the October 1888 term of U.S. District Court at Graham, a grand jury impaneled by Judge McCormick found separate indictments numbered 235, 236 and 239 against Boone, Epp and Alf Marlow, respectively as follows:

That on the 7th day of March 1855 . . . BOONE MARLOW . . . in the Kiowa, Comanche and Wichita Agency, Indian Territory . . . did fraudulently and feloniously take, steal and carry away and appropriate to his own use and benefit Ten Mares of the value of Thirty Dollars each, five Geldings of the value of Thirty Dollars each, two horses of the value of Fifty Dollars each, one filly of the value of Twenty Dollars, and one foal of the value of Ten Dollars, said animals being then and there the property of Ba-Sinda-Bar, a Caddo Indian. . . .[16]

That on the 16th day of March 1885 . . . EPP MAR-LOW . . . in the Kiowa, Comanche and Wichita Agency, Indian Territory . . . did fraudulently and feloniously take, steal and carry away and appropriate to his own use and benefit Nine Mares of the value of Twenty-eight Dollars each, six Geldings and two fillies of the value of Thirty Dollars each, and two foals of the value of Ten Dollars each, said animals of the horse species, being then and there the property of Ba-Sinda-Bar, a Caddo Indian. . . .[17]

That on the 10th day of March 1885 . . . ALF MAR-LOW . . . in the Kiowa, Comanche and Wichita Agency, Indian Territory . . . did fraudulently and feloniously take, steal and carry away and appropriate to his own use and benefit Five Mares of the value of Thirty Dollars each, three fillies of the value of Twenty-five Dollars each, and one foal of the value of Fifteen Dollars, said animals of the equine species, being then and there the property of Ba-Sinda-Bar, a Caddo Indian. . . .[18]

All three indictments listed as government witnesses: Ba-Sinda-Bar, Indian; J. W. Murphy; Mrs. Patsy Johnson; Seth Huntley; James Graves; Joe Fadder, Indian; Charles Keel, Indian; and Dus-chet, Indian.

Boone, Epp and Alf were arraigned in commissioner's court to answer the indictments on October 9. Witness Murphy could not be located, and Indians Fadder, Keel and Dus-chet refused to cooperate. Johnson also had trouble with the Indian victims.

The indictments showed a total of seventy-six horses, mares, fillies and foals stolen from Ba-Sinda-Bar, none of which had been recovered. Ba-Sinda-Bar testified that he did not "own that many horses"; that "Marlow men no steal

Indian man's horses anyway, because he [they] have better horses he [they] get somewhere else, but Indian man thinks these white mans steal [meaning Johnson, Allen and Criswell] if Indian man don't sleep with one eye open." Black Crow, the Comanche, and Washington, the Caddo, also doubted that the Marlows had taken their ponies. Sunday Boy wanted to pledge all of his lands and squaws for Charles' and Alf's freedom, and the other Indians offered as much. Commissioner Girand informed them that it was unlawful to take an Indian on a white man's bond.[19]

Boone, Epp and Alf admitted being in the Fort Sill country in March 1885 when Ba-Sinda-Bar's horses were stolen, but they had only been passing through with their family en route to Texas prior to Dr. Marlow's death near Wichita Falls in April 1885. Nor could they have stolen the horses of Black Crow and Washington between January and March 1886; they were still in No Man's Land. Also, they could furnish the time and place of purchase of the horses and mules George and their mother had brought to Graham from Anadarko, none of which had been claimed by anyone as stolen property.[20]

Nonetheless, the defendants were bound over to district court. Arraigned before Judge McCormick, Boone, Alf and Epp entered pleas of not guilty and were recommitted for trial at the March 1889 term. Attorney Arnold applied for writs of habeas corpus, which Judge McCormick denied on October 10, and continued bail in the amount of $500 each. George Marlow, his case pending in U.S. commissioner's court, remained in jail in lieu of bond.

Then the Spartan nature of Martha Marlow showed itself. She went out among the Young County farmers and gained the release of her sons by giving the horses brought from Anadarko as security. On October 29, O. G. Denson, D. C. Brooks and Frank Herron "jointly and severally" pledged their land, buildings and personal property as bail for Charles and Alf; J. D. Short stood for George and Epp.[21]

Charles and Alf, with their wives and mother, moved into a

log and clapboard structure on the Denson farm fifteen miles southeast of Graham, near the Jack County line, and began planting wheat. George and Epp rented a place a few miles away and went to work for Short.

On Saturday, December 15, Denson made bail for Boone. Boone spent that night with George at the Short place and the next day went down to the Denson farm to stay with Charles and Alf.

The five brothers thought their troubles were over for a while, but they were just beginning.

George recalled: "We ceased to fear Johnson because of the reputation of the man in general. Some of the best citizens expressed their opinion that he amounted to very little as a man of honor. Among these was Sheriff Wallace. . . .

"Mr. Wallace was a popular man . . . had treated us kindly while we were in his care, and not one of us would have intentionally harmed him. . . . After our release, he was a frequent visitor at our homes, and expressed himself thusly:

"'Johnson will let you alone after he gets all your stock and money. He's not apt to molest a poor man. Yes,' he continued, as he seemed to recollect some past villainy of Johnson's, 'the infernal rascal has forged many a warrant to make a few dimes.'"[22]

Some of Wallace's enmity stemmed from a clash with the deputy marshal at Jeffrey's Saloon in Graham one afternoon following the arrest of the Marlows. Jeffrey's was a popular loafing place and a center for business and professional sociality. Wallace and Johnson were having a drink, with a goodly crowd present, when the question arose about Johnson's left-handed marksmanship.

Wallace was a great hand to joke, but Johnson took his remark as an insult. His temper flared. He allowed that he could hit a dime on a tree at twenty paces, three times out of four. A dozen or more men quickly placed bets, and the crowd repaired to the edge of town for the shoot.

Wallace placed a dime on a tree about five feet above the

ground. Johnson requested that it be placed near the roots. Wallace argued that its position had not been mentioned beforehand, and Johnson called him a liar. Wallace reached for his .45, but Johnson was quicker, and the sheriff dropped his half-drawn weapon back in the holster.

Friends counseled both men and the bets were withdrawn. Whereupon Johnson placed a dime at the roots of the tree and hit it three shots out of four to prove his boast. But the misunderstanding had not been forgotten.

Johnson obviously feared a loss of face because of the flimsy evidence presented to the grand jury. Following the indictments of the Marlows, he continued to circulate the report that they were "bad men" and, to show the cattlemen he meant business, he brought five more prisoners to the Graham jail. Three were from Indian Territory — one "an old violator he had been on the lookout for a long time" and two charged with horse stealing — and the fourth a cattle rustler from Wilbarger County named Murphy (missing witness J. W. Murphy?), "who would testify against the Marlows."[23]

While in Wilbarger County arresting Murphy, Johnson and Sam Criswell stirred up the Holdson case. A state warrant charging Boone Marlow with murder, on which Johnson and Criswell appeared as witnesses, was sent to Young County.[24]

IV

"Damn You, Tom Collier!"

Sheriff Marion Wallace received the warrant from Wilbarger County on Monday morning, December 17 — the second day after Boone was released on bail — and went to the Denson place, accompanied by his chief deputy, tall, droopy-mustached Thomas B. "Tom" Collier. The officers reached the Marlow cabin about twelve o'clock, rode to the chimney end where there was no door or window, and dismounted.

Alf Marlow was at Denson's house several hundred yards away. George and his family were at the Short farm. Inside the cabin, Charles and his wife, Alf's wife, Martha Marlow, Epp and Boone had just sat down to their noon meal. The table was by the window on the west side of the room and opposite the door. Epp sat with his back to the door, Charles at the north end of the table, and Boone at the south end next to a

Deputy Sheriff Thomas B. "Tom" Collier.

bed in the southwest corner of the room, on which lay a Winchester rifle.

None of the cabin's occupants were aware of either officer's presence until Collier peered in the window.

Boone saw him first, and called: "Hello, Tom. Come in and have some dinner."

"I'm not hungry," Collier replied.

"Come in anyway," Boone said.

Collier walked around the cabin as though accepting the invitation and opened the door. As Boone rose to welcome him, the deputy paused with one foot on the threshold, and drew his revolver.

"I've come for you, Boone," he said, and fired.

Boone ducked and seized the Winchester from the bed. The women screamed. Collier, seeing he had missed his man, jumped back to close the door. Boone's bullet grazed his temple, ripped the brim of his hat, and splintered the door casing. As the deputy dodged from the doorway, Boone fired again.

Sheriff Wallace, hearing Collier's shot and the screams, dashed around the cabin and had just stepped up behind his deputy. Boone's second bullet caught him above the right hip and passed through his body. He fell backward and collapsed on the porch.

Charles Marlow stated: "Epp and I jumped from the table and rushed to the door, saw Wallace. It was the first time we knew he was on the place. We spoke to him and he asked me to come and hold his head up. I went out and put his head on my lap.

"Boone called for Collier to come back. He came back and dropped his gun. Boone kept his rifle on him, and said, 'Damn you, Tom Collier, you fired on me like I was a dog,' and Collier said, 'I know, but let's not say anything more about it.' Boone said to me, 'Charley, I want to shoot him between the eyes — he is the cause of this,' and Collier clung to me and begged me not to let Boone kill him. I told Boone to put down his gun.

"Collier got his horse and rode off. He had said nothing to Boone about having a warrant for him. Nothing was said about any papers before the fight. . . ."[1]

Denson had heard the gunfire at his house, and he and Alf rushed to the scene. They removed Wallace's coat, hung it on the porch, then carried the sheriff inside and placed him on a pallet.

Wallace told Denson that Collier was "justified" in what he had done. "If you will look in my coat pocket, you will find a capias for Boone." Denson found the warrant — "in a bundle of papers, a good large bundle tied up with a string several times around it."[2]

Every care was given Sheriff Wallace by the women. Martha Marlow "kept talking to him and rubbing his feet and legs — he was complaining about his feet and legs all the time."[3]

Epp rode to the Short farm, told George what had happened and that he was going to Graham for a doctor. George went to the Denson place with J. D. Short. Two physicians finally arrived, but without Epp. Epp, they explained, had been arrested by Wallace's office deputy tax collector, John Levell.

Two county prisoners with cases pending, John F. Speer and Sam Burns, saw Levell "bring Epp in. . . . Epp objected to being put in jail, saying he had done nothing wrong . . . only come for a doctor and to let Wallace's friends know he had been shot, and Levell, cursing him, said, 'Go in there, and we will mob the rest.' Levell then kicked Epp into the cage."[4]

The *Graham Leader* of December 20 said: "At two o'clock last Monday, our town was thrown into feverish excitement by the report that our Sheriff had been shot, perhaps fatally, by Boone Marlow. . . . Every man who could procure a horse and a six-shooter or a Winchester immediately repaired to the Denson place. . . ."

The physicians could do little for Wallace except stop his bleeding. He was placed on their hack and rushed back to Graham.

Collier returned to the scene a few minutes later, "a crowd at his back," among them D. C. Brooks and Frank Herron. After a brief conference with Denson and Short, the four bondsmen agreed "to give up the Marlows to Collier" and be released as sureties. Collier "gave the brothers to understand that they were again prisoners." George, Charles, and Alf joined Epp in the Young County jail, leaving their mother and wives "to get by any way they could, alone."[5]

Boone had vanished. The *Leader* report of December 20 continued:

> Sheriff G[eorge] W. Moore immediately summoned a posse of Jack County citizens and . . . placed himself and his men under the orders of Young County authorities. He is now scouring the woods. . . . It is the intention of the officers to leave no stone unturned in the search for the culprit, who is thought to be hiding in the cedar brakes south of the Brazos. . . .
>
> Sheriff [John J.] Douglas, with a posse from Stephens County, arrived in Graham Tuesday night to join in the search.
>
> It is gratifying to see Wallace's brother officers thus coming to our assistance in the hour of need.

George Moore, a farmer and stock raiser elected sheriff of Jack County in November 1888, summarized his part in the manhunt:

"Bruce Wheeler, whom I've known a long time, came after me. Said he wanted me to assist in capturing Boone Marlow and bring everyone I could get. I brought a dozen or so men, maybe 18 or 20. I met Eugene Logan at the Denson farm. . . . [Logan lived in Belknap and ranched on the Brazos; he was constable of the Belknap precinct and acted as a deputy under Wallace.] Logan was with P. A. Martin, Tom Collier and several others.

"Collier told me he did not know who shot Wallace, that it

might have been Charley Marlow instead of Boone. Said the Marlows asked him to get his dinner, that Wallace walked to the southeast of the house, and he [Collier] heard the firing. He ran around to the door as Wallace was shot, and Wallace told him to run. Collier said he ran out in the yard and the Marlows called him to come back and wait on Wallace, which he did. . . .

"The other Marlows, or some of them, had been arrested. I never knew what for, but supposed they were accessories to the shooting. . . . I went southwest to the Clear Fork [of the Brazos], then to Graham, and northeast to Antelope. I hunted for Boone Marlow about two days and a half. Logan was with me a part of two days. He seemed to be moved the same as I was, with a desire to arrest Boone. . . . We did not even hear of Boone, so I quit the search at Antelope, went on down to Post Oak, and from there back to Jacksboro."[6]

In *Life of the Marlows*, George and Charles explained how Boone eluded the pursuit.[7] The county swarmed with men eager for his scalp, by fair means or foul. Boone tunnelled into a big stack of wheat straw half a mile from Denson's house, excavating a room big enough for all practical purposes. Charles' wife Emma brought him food daily under a cover of darkness, always taking different routes through the woods, and kept him posted on guards or posses prowling around. George's wife Lillian moved from the Short farm to be with the rest of the women and share the sorrow and distress which had fallen upon them all. Time after time, the officials overhauled everything on the place and the cabin. Not a box, trunk, closet or drawer escaped their pilfering. They poked under the beds with their guns and tore up the floor under pretense of looking for Boone, but more to irritate the women than anything else. Several volumes of medical books Martha Marlow had kept in remembrance of her husband were tumbled about until she, with the help of Emma and Lillian, dug a deep hole one night in the bed of a ravine and buried them, preferring that they decay rather than be polluted by the touch of insolent blood-hunters. After staying in the straw stack for days, Boone changed his hiding place to an old corn crib filled with fodder close to the cabin. It already had been examined by a posse. He intended to take vengeance on the next man he saw harassing the women. From there he could command all that transpired and felt pretty safe. But Lillian thought it was too risky. She went to the pasture where the Marlow horses were kept and told Denson she needed a mount to make a trip to Graham. Denson obliged. She chose Epp's big black horse and also took Epp's saddle. About ten o'clock that night, Boone came out of the corn blades to run the gauntlet. Martha Marlow gave him an overcoat, a muffler, and her testament. Then he kissed the women goodbye and rode off to the grounds he knew so well in Indian Territory. Next morning Lillian told Denson she had tied the horse to a wagon in the yard, intending to start early for Graham, but the animal had worked itself loose and possibly was feeding somewhere in the neighborhood. Of course, Denson failed to find the horse. If he suspected that she was deceiving him, he never made it known by word or action; he reported the horse stolen by some party or parties unknown.

On December 17, at the behest of Tom Collier and John Levell, County Attorney Martin telegraphed Governor Sul Ross at Austin that Sheriff Wallace had been mortally wounded by Boone Marlow and asked him to offer a reward for his capture. Governor Ross authorized $200 to be paid "on condition of the arrest and return of said fugitive within six months . . . and conviction thereafter."[8] Martin received the governor's proclamation on December 22. Dissatisfied citizens promptly added $1,500, payable upon Boone's delivery to Young County authorities, "dead or alive." All of which the *Leader* of December 27 headlined: "$1,700 REWARD! Let all good citizens turn out and assist in his capture. He is well armed and will no doubt resist to the last."

Sheriff Wallace lingered at his home in "precarious condition." The bullet had passed through his kidneys, and many believed he would "surely die." Physicians pointed to his "most indomitable pluck and iron constitution," and "held hopes for his recovery." In his hours of consciousness, he "spoke of his friends who stood by his side and assured them that he would again be well . . . but, when the dread delirium came on he seemed to take up his work again, and his detective instinct led him upon the imaginitive trail of his murderer. . . ." He died at ten o'clock in the morning on Monday, December 24, and was buried on Christmas day.[9]

The day Wallace died, the Marlow bondsmen surrendered the brothers before Commissioner Girand. Girand discharged them as sureties, declared Boone a federal fugitive, and remanded George, Charles, Alf and Epp to the custody of the United States marshal to answer their existing indictments. Deputy Johnson returned them to the Young County jail in default of bail of $100 each.[10]

The Young County commissioners named Tom Collier to complete the term of Sheriff Wallace. Collier then appointed "Little Marion" A. Wallace as deputy, and Marion A. became "much about the jail in relation to the custody of the Marlows and other prisoners."[11] Constable Samuel V. "Sam" Waggoner of Graham township and Constable Eugene Logan were also appointed as deputy sheriffs. John Levell, who boarded at the Wallace home with Little Marion, was retained in his post as office deputy and collector of taxes.

Collier made bond as sheriff and was qualified on Friday, December 28. "He seems to be the choice of the people," said the *Leader* of that date, "and we confidently predict that Deputy Sheriff Marion A. Wallace will prove worthy of the trust confided to him. . . ."

Collier's first act was to appease complaining taxpayers. As *ex-officio* collector of taxes, he posted the following notice:

> As the death of Mr. Wallace rendered it impossible for anyone to pay taxes for several days . . . I have decided to extend the time for payment to January 29th. No cost will be assessed against anyone until after that date.[12]

Collier's next move was to charge George, Charles, Alf and Epp with complicity in the murder of Sheriff Wallace. He disregarded the fact that George had been at the Short farm and a report by one Marion Lasater, which verified the brothers' version of the affair.

Lasater was a prominent Young County citizen — a Scotsman, tall and graceful, with searching clear blue eyes that could twinkle with merriment when occasion offered or blaze and sparkle at an injustice. He was among the first arrivals at the Denson place and had examined the inside of the cabin:

"I found two bullet holes, one in the west wall [Collier's shot], the other inside the door . . . three or four inches from the edge where it had cut through the facing and had been fired from inside the house, the way the casing was splintered. The door opened toward the inside of the house . . . seemed [to have been] standing not quite half open when the shot was fired. The bullet hole was about as high as my cheek from the floor . . . I did not see Marion Wallace's wound, but this shot must have come from inside the house, also."[13]

County Attorney Martin admitted that he "did not know enough facts to make the complaint" against the Marlows, but "made it anyway."[14] The *Leader* said: "It is the theory of the State that they [George, Charles, Alf and Epp] were present, aiding and abetting in the offense, if not actual participants." The defense contended that it was a clear case of persecution; that Boone did the shooting without advice or assistance of his brothers.

Justice J. S. Sterrett, sitting as examining magistrate on December 31, gave the Marlows until January 4 to procure additional testimony in their behalf; he set bail at $1,000 each, which they were unable to make, and on motion of County Attorney Martin, remanded them to jail as state prisoners.[15]

V

"They All Ought to be Killed"

The death of Sheriff Wallace intensified the feeling in Young County against the Marlows. Tom Collier, chafing under his failure to capture Boone, took advantage of the prevailing mood. He virtually "joined hands" with Marion A. Wallace, John Levell, Sam Waggoner, Eugene Logan, Sam Criswell and others in "constantly expressing fear that the brothers would be taken from the jail and lynched."[1]

George, Charles, Alf and Epp were confined separately from the other prisoners, given food of the "coarsest kind and not enough to have satisfied the hunger of one man, much less four stalwarts like themselves," and were denied any communication with their mother, wives and former bondsmen. Attorney Arnold withdrew from their case, apparently for lack of additional fees he requested. The turnkey and jail guards "seemed intent on making their existence miserable by heaping upon them insults, taunts and indignities," and discussed openly the rumors of mob action. Deputy Johnson showed little concern for their plight, though they were also federal prisoners. Convinced that they could not get justice in the Graham courts, they "resolved to make a break for liberty."[2]

The jail was of stone construction. There were four rooms on the ground floor which were used for an office, the turnkey's quarters, and other official business. A narrow, winding stairway led to the jail room or upper story. At the head of the stairs, a steel door, set in the stone wall, opened into a three-by-four-foot anteroom. Another steel door opened from the anteroom into the prison area, which contained two cages, one on the north side and one on the south side of the room, each approximately sixteen feet long and seven feet wide, with grated door and sides of sheet iron. There was a water closet just off the anteroom and a corridor or run-around between the cages, from which could be seen the portion of the stairway that turned from the ground floor. The Marlows were confined in the south cage.

In the north cage languished federal prisoners Louis Clift and W. D. Burkhart, who were awaiting transfer to the Western District of Arkansas at Fort Smith, and county prisoners Speer and Burns, charged with horse stealing and theft of a saddle, respectively. When incarcerated, Speer had managed to conceal a large pocket knife, which he stuck into the end of a broom handle and poked through the bars of his cage across the corridor to the Marlows.

The brothers took turns each night working with the knife on the metal wall of the cage, concealing their handiwork with a blanket in the daytime. It was a slow, tedious process, but they were strong and determined. It took them a week to cut an opening large enough to crawl through.

Monday night, January 14, after the turnkey had checked the prisoners and retired, the Marlows ripped their blankets into long strips, wove them into a rope, and lowered themselves quickly and silently into the jailyard. No outside guards were on duty. They had three hours start when Sheriff Collier came to the jail to make a final check before going to bed himself and discovered they were missing. The ground was muddy from recent rains and the escapees left a plain trail in the direction of the Brazos. Collier and Johnson, with half a dozen heavily armed possemen, set out in direct pursuit and sent Deputy Wallace and Marion Lasater to watch the Marlow cabin on the Denson farm.[3]

Lasater had talked with Collier "nearly every day about the Marlows. I told him I would assist him at any time, but I was never asked to help out at the jail."[4]

George Marlow described their flight and capture: "The night was cold. We had no wraps and went as straight for our home as we could get there. The Brazos was up, and we waited all night to cross. We were within half a mile of our home at daybreak when we saw the posse below in the trees. They came dashing up with rifles and revolvers drawn, and Collier yelled, 'Throw away your guns, or be killed!' I told him to shut up or I would knock him off his horse with a rock — 'You know we don't have any guns.' We surrendered to Johnson and were taken to Short's farm, put in a wagon and brought back to town. We were taken to a blacksmith shop and shackled together, two and two — Charley and Alf, me and Epp — by irons riveted around one leg each connected by a chain. Then we were locked in jail, this time in the north cage with Speer, Burns, Clift and Burkhart. 'Now, damn you,' Collier said, 'I guess you'll not get away again.'"[5]

Lasater described the knife used in the escape: "It was three-bladed once . . . one blade was broken off. The large blade was made into a kind of saw. The little blade had been rounded off and made into a gimlet [for boring holes]. We did not get the knife when the Marlows were arrested. Afterwards, I found it under a rock on the Brazos, about a hundred yards above the mouth of Conner Creek. . . . George told me where it was."[6]

George claimed the knife, but "somehow Collier learned it was Speer's. Collier told Speer 'I will not iron you — you have done nobody harm in Young County and are in no danger — but I swear to you that the Marlows will catch hell.' About mid-afternoon, Collier returned to the jail, stating, 'The county commissioners have ordered me to iron you and Burkhart.' Speer and Burkhart were chained together."[7]

As sentiment against the Marlows mounted, Collier boasted that, by acting quickly, he and his men had prevented them from obtaining weapons and horses, fleeing the country and joining the murdering Boone. Charles stated: "The officers who had in the beginning started out to ruin us . . . actuated by the hope of gain and personal aggrandizement . . . spread abroad every lie and innuendo which could suggest itself to their scheming minds."[8]

Several Young County citizens perceived the possibility if not the probability of a lynching.

A. B. Gant paid his taxes the day of the capture and heard John Levell remark that the Marlows could not be convicted "on the evidence officers had" and a mob seemed "a reasonable solution."[9]

That same afternoon, one Bailey Allen saw Eugene Logan and William Williams (commonly known as "Bee" Williams) standing on the east side of the public square, "apart from all other persons and engaged in earnest private conversation." Bee was the son of "Uncle Harry" Williams, an ex-Confederate soldier and noted frontiersman who had fought Indians in Texas before and after the Civil War and served as first county clerk at Belknap. For more than an hour during the prosecution of his work, Allen passed Logan and Williams several time and "observed them in the same place, similarly engaged." It so challenged his attention that he commented to friends, "Something must be up."[10]

Wednesday evening, January 16, Collier and Sam Waggoner appeared on some mission at Bryson, in Jack County, twelve miles northeast of Graham. While Collier was in the hotel ordering supper, Waggoner talked to Bryson residents Dick Smith and Walter Hamilton about the Marlows, stating, "There ought to be a mob gotten up to make way with them."[11]

A similar discussion was underway the same evening at the boardinghouse of Mrs. R. C. Lauderdale in Belknap. Mrs. Lauderdale was the mother-in-law of Sam Criswell. Criswell and her daughter, Dixie, lived with her. Mrs. Lauderdale deposed: "Eugene Logan, Will Benedict and Bee Williams were in my room talking with Sam about the Marlows. . . . Sam said old lady Marlow had raised her sons to be murderers and horse thieves and they all ought to be killed. Williams said they ought to be mobbed and that he was willing to help at any time. Benedict said something about breaking in the jail and killing them right off — 'If they are turned loose they will burn the town.' Logan thought that if the Marlows were as mean as the others said, they would have killed Tom Collier when they shot Wallace — 'They could have done it.'"[12]

In Graham, Marion Lasater was hearing "a right smart talk" about a mob: "Peter Harmonson came to me and asked if I would help keep it down. He did not tell me who had been talking to him [but] as we were talking Bruce Wheeler and W. O. Clark passed along the street and Harmonson said, 'There goes two men who have abused their conscience. . . . [Wheeler was a young cattleman who ranched with Clark in the Olney community.] I went up to the saloon where Bruce Wheeler was talking to W. R. Bigham . . . Bigham took a dollar and flipped it up and said 'Let's go in and have a drink.' I did not want to go, and neither did Wheeler, and after Bigham went in, I told Wheeler that I did not believe those boys ought to be mobbed. He said he thought they ought. . . ."[13]

Lasater discussed his concerns with Postmaster John Taylor and the town's founder, Edwin S. Graham. Graham and Taylor were "so impressed with this apprehension that they went to the home of Commissioner Girand at night [January

16], after he had gone to bed, and got him to advise the deputy marshal [Johnson] that the Marlows might be attacked." Johnson assured Girand that the prisoners were being closely guarded by Collier and his deputies, "some of them staying up all the time."[14]

There was an even more pertinent development on Thursday evening, January 17, at the home of the Widow Wallace. Deputies Marion Wallace and John Levell ate supper there and returned to the jail about six o'clock. A Mrs. Rickman, who lived across the road and a short distance north of Mrs. Wallace, dropped in to visit soon after supper and stayed until fifteen minutes past nine. She recalled: "A few minutes before nine o'clock Tom Collier came in and told Mrs. Wallace he was nearly dead for sleep, that he had not slept for four days, and asked if he could have a bed that night. [Collier usually slept at the jail]. Mrs. Wallace said he could but wished he would first go to the jail and see how Marion was getting along. Collier said Marion was all right and he wanted to go to bed, but Mrs. Wallace insisted, and he went out. I do not know whether he went to the jail or to the horse lot to put up his horse. . . . Soon after he left, Sam Waggoner came and asked for him, and being told that Collier had just gone, Waggoner went out. Then Collier came back and told Mrs. Wallace he had to go after a fellow he had been wanting to get for some time, named Vance; that he knew where Vance was then and if he waited until tomorrow, Vance would be gone. Collier left again. . . . During the evening, I saw three men out by the cistern that I did not know. I saw several others about the premises. . . . At 9:15 my son came for me and I remarked to him as we started home that I did not understand what it meant, and he said, 'It's nothing, Ma. Don't you know they are guarding the jail?'"[15]

Shortly before midnight, about fifteen disguised and armed men entered Graham's little bastille, allegedly took the guards into custody, and stormed upstairs to seize the prisoners. The *Leader* of January 24, 1889, erroneously set the time at 3:00

A. M., January 18, gave the number in the mob at "about forty," and reported the action as follows:

> All the guards were asleep but one. . . . The first warn-
> ing the guards had of their presence was the opening of
> the door and the pointing of a dozen or more guns at
> their heads, with a demand to surrender — a demand
> with which they readily complied. Then the mob made
> them go up and open the cages and call all the prisoners
> out except the Marlows. They then attempted to get
> them out of the cage, but met with a bold stand-off.
> One of the Marlows wrenched off a piece of iron water
> pipe, with which he defended the door, and, after a par-
> ley of a few minutes, the mob beat a retreat in good
> order. As they retired they took the guards with
> them . . . led two of the guards with ropes . . . down to
> the graveyard [cemetery about one hundred yards from
> the jail], where they released them and silently stole
> away. . . . It is a matter of wonder that they did not
> shoot the prisoners in the cage. . . . Who they were and
> where from are matters of conjecture. The guards failed
> to recognize any of them.

However, Charles and George Marlow, Burns and Speer would testify that they recognized Eugene P. Logan, P. A. Martin, Sam Criswell, Dick Cook (a day guard at the jail), Will Benedict, Pink Brooks, Clint Rutherford, Frank Harmison, Vernon "Verna" Wilkerson and Bob Hill. Hill was the brash young son of the respected Hill family that lived seven miles from Graham. Harmison ranched on the Archer-Young county line. Wilkerson ranched in the northern part of Young County and lived nine miles north of Graham, on Farmer Road.

All the mob members wore "old clothes, or fancy and *outre* style dress, by way of disguises." Cook "had an old knit cap pulled down over his forehead," but was "easily recognized by having only three fingers on one hand." Cook "stayed right at the window of the cage by Pink Brooks," whose face was "blackened around and under they eyes." Martin "had a handkerchief tied over his face with a big eye-hole cut in it, and carried a lantern." Logan "had a handkerchief tied over his face below the eyes," and wore "copper colored breeches with a split place in the left knee." Logan had torn his trousers during the Monday night hunt for the Marlows, and Charles had kidded him, "If we get out of jail again, you will have to get some more breeches." Logan was armed with a Winchester and "took a commanding and leading part in what was said and done."[16]

The Marlows, Burns and Speer would further testify about details of the attack, as follows:

No light was allowed in the jail, and the prisoners had been "ordered to bed at dark." A few hours later, Speer was awakened by a party knocking on the ground floor door — "I heard someone inside ask, 'Who is it?' and the party on the outside said, 'It's me.' The guards then opened the door, and I woke the other prisoners. We heard several voices 'hallooing,' then ten or twelve men crowded upstairs." John Levell was in the lead, swinging his keys and a lantern. "Martin had the other lantern," which he hung in the corridor. Levell unlocked the door of the north cage, and called, "Charley, come out here; someone wants to see you." Speer said, "Charley, don't go, that is a mob; don't you see they are disguised?" Charles asked, "What do they want?" and Levell replied, "Come out and see." Charles said, "I can't come out without Alf — we're chained together." George "knew that the mob thirsted especially for Charley's blood, for Collier had spread the report that Charley instead of Boone had killed Sheriff Wallace," and he said, "Boys, don't go." George told Levell, "John, I would not have thought you would do this . . . we have laid up here till ten or eleven o'clock at night begging for water, and you would say that the keys were down at the [sheriff's] office, but you can get the keys to let these fellows in." Logan punched George in the side with his Winchester, and said, "Shut up" when half a dozen guns were poked through the cracks in the cage. The longer the talk continued, the louder the mob cursed. Young Bob Hill, tired of the delay, "made a rush into the cage to push Charley out." Charles caught him with a powerful left to the chin, knocking him back into the corridor, where he fell and his head struck the stone wall. He lay on the floor groaning, and the mob fell back in dismay. Finally, Hill gasped, "Frank [meaning Harmison], take me out of here — I'm bleeding to death!" Harmison and another man picked him up and carried him downstairs. George and Epp hobbled to the side of Charles and Alf, and the four stood waiting, "resolved to die fighting." The mob "did not dare arouse the town by shooting." Logan ordered Levell to "lock up," and all went downstairs with Harmison and Bob Hill. (The Hills kept their son's injury very quiet; he died at home a few days later, the cause of his death reported as "inflamation of the brain.")[17]

The Marlow-Burns-Speer testimony continued:

Within a few minutes, the mob returned to the jail, Deputy Marion Wallace in the lead. "Martin hung his lantern in the same place." Clift had screwed off a joint of lead water pipe that went through to the water closet and handed it to Alf. Burns said, "Wallace unlocked the door, and they called us out — me, Speer, Clift and Burkhart — and put us in the south cage. Then Harmison told Wallace to go in and bring Charley out. Wallace started in the cage, saw Alf standing with that pipe ready to brain anybody who entered, and jumped back, saying, 'I'll be damned if I'm going in there to be killed.' Someone — I think it was Bruce Wheeler — said, 'I will bring him out.' He ran downstairs, got a lariat, and tried to lasso Charley in the cage, but couldn't do anything with it [the rope]." There were men in the mob as tough as the Marlows, but they "heeded Charley's action against Hill and the pipe in the hands of Alf." They "blustered and argued for a time." Then Wallace locked the cage door, and all departed.

Speer said, "After the mob left, Clift crawled out of the hole the Marlows had cut in the cage to escape and said he was going down town to let the people know how we were being treated, but he saw the guards coming upstairs and got back in the cage. The guards claimed the mob had put ropes around their necks and took them to the graveyard and released them. I told them, 'You fellows haven't had time to get to the graveyard yet.'" George stated that "both Wallace and Levell came up that trip, Logan and Criswell with them, their disguises removed. They came up to the door, and I asked if they intended to kill us. They laughed and said they had scared the mob away. Logan stepped to the corner of the cage, and said, 'We have got you damned sons-of-bitches off.' I told him I was glad. They asked if we had recognized any of the mob, and we denied knowing that they were the same parties. The boys and I already had talked it over, hoping by that course to secure our own safety. They took Burns, Speer, Clift and Burkhart out of the south cage and put them back in the north cage with us, then went back downstairs. We did not lay down anymore that night — just sat up talking."[18]

VI

"You Lied to Us, Ed"

Immediately after the mob's departure, the town was aroused by a report that a gang of desperadoes from Indian Territory, led by Boone Marlow, had tried to capture the jail and rescue his brothers but had been foiled by Sheriff Collier's faithful guards and deputies. However, four ropes with nooses, discovered in the cemetery at daybreak and obviously intended for the Marlows, gave lie to this fabrication.[1]

Many substantial citizens of Graham demanded an investigation, and Joseph W. Graves echoed their sentiments in a *Leader* editorial on January 24:

> When prisoners are placed in jail, disarmed and shackled, the laws of our state guarantee to them protection from mob violence and a fair and impartial trial for their

offenses, whatever they may be. . . . These men confined here are a desperate set of ruffians, but still they are entitled to the full benefit of the law. . . .

It is thought by some that [the mob] did not intend to hang anyone, but simply to frighten them. No matter what the plan was, it was a dismal failure, and doubtless the would-be executioners went home heartily ashamed of their night's work, fully realizing that they had made a most complete fiasco and done themselves and the country no good. . . .

Alibis for those known to have supported lynching the Marlows came thick and fast.

County Attorney Martin slept in a room on the third story of the courthouse and claimed to have been in bed at the time the jail was attacked. He "remembered" that Sam Waggoner came to him "around nine o'clock and made a complaint against eighteen-year-old Jimmy Vance for carrying a pistol. I made an information, and we went down into the county clerk's office and got a warrant. . . . I do not think I saw Collier, but he may have been in the clerk's office. . . ."[2]

County Clerk A. T. Gay, who slept in the courthouse on the second floor, "filed the complaint and issued the capias," then returned to bed.[3]

Martin claimed he also had returned to bed; that sometime after midnight he was awakened by "a noise in the court room below, and after I got down into the court room, I found Mr. Gay and Marion Wallace. I asked what was the matter, and Marion told me the jail had been attacked. I went to the jail then and stayed till morning. . . . I did not make any effort to discover who the mob was that attacked the jail. I sent a telegram to the state district attorney, and he advised me that a secret investigation would be better when the grand jury met. . . . It was not a very long time until our winter term of court began, so I let the matter alone. . . . Judge Sterrett showed me a letter from the district attorney afterwards, giving him like advice."[4]

Collier and Waggoner claimed they knew nothing of the affair. They had gone several miles from Graham after obtaining the warrant, attempting to apprehend young Vance.

John Putman and his wife, who lived six miles west of Graham and about a mile from Jimmy Vance's widowed mother, saw the two officers at their gate around midnight. Putman "got up and brought them inside . . . said they were cold. I took them into the kitchen and started a fire . . . asked if they would not strip their horses and put them up and go to bed till morning, and they said no, that their horses were too warm. The horses appeared to have been ridden hard. Said they had come out to arrest Vance, but did not get him, and would have to be back in Graham by sunup. Mrs. Putman prepared an early breakfast, and they left about daylight."[5]

Martin claimed that Jimmy Vance was arrested later and his case was dismissed. However, Mrs. Vance, who was well acquainted with Collier and Waggoner, declared "they were never at my house to arrest my son. I never saw them anywhere on the night of January 17th." Upon hearing that a warrant had been issued for her son, she "came to the courthouse and examined the books, without finding record of it."[6]

Strangely, Jimmy Vance was known to have left Young County with a cattle herd on January 13. And government prosecutors later questioned the logic of a sheriff and his deputy, much needed because of the probability of mob action, riding off in the night to arrest a youth carrying a pistol.

Upon returning to Graham, Collier brought Speer from the jail and asked if he knew who was in the mob. Speer said, "I told him I did not know. I was satisfied that he knew all about the mob and that they would kill me if I knew who was in it. Tom Collier heard I had a list, and said if I had, I better destroy it — it was no use for me to throw my life away for the Marlows.

"Robert Holman also asked me about it and wanted to know what I would swear to in the Marlow cases. Said he would have me pardoned. . . . Wallace, Levell, Logan and some others searched the prison area. Wallace recovered the water closet pipe, held it up, and said to Alf, 'This is what you intended to kill me with last night.' George spoke up, 'We would have protected you better than you have protected us,' and Wallace flushed at the remark."[7]

Logan claimed to have been a guard at the jail when he mob attacked. However, Postmaster Taylor noted "the *levity* Logan indulged in when relating the occurrence" to him.[8]

Logan asked the Marlows if they could describe any of the mob members. Charles replied, "They were the tallest men we ever saw," and Logan laughed and repeated, "Yes, the tallest men you ever did see."[9]

Attorney Arnold dropped by to see the Marlows. They asked if he could have them removed from Graham, and Arnold told them they were Collier's prisoners.

Marion Lasater called attention to their federal status: "For some reason I was not informed of the mob until after sunup. I talked to a good many people about it, and I talked to Ed Johnson. I asked Johnson if he was going to let these boys be killed. I told him if I were in his place, I would go to the jail and protect them . . . then I would kill the next man who tried anything. He said he would telegraph Marshal Cabell what to do."[10]

Saturday morning, January 19, Marshal Cabell telegraphed Johnson to remove all federal prisoners in the Young County jail to the Parker County jail, at Weatherford, for safekeeping. Weatherford was some sixty miles overland from Graham. The order included Clift and Burkhart and was to be carried out at once, under heavy guard, and with the utmost secrecy.

Johnson consulted U.S. Commissioner Girand. They decided, in light of sharply divided public opinion, that some of the guards should be obtained from among the friends of the deceased Sheriff Wallace, to prevent them stirring up further violence. Girand named Marion Wallace, Sam Waggoner and John Levell. Johnson chose Sam Criswell, John B. Girand (the commissioner's twenty-two-year-old son), and Will

Hollis of Belknap. All agreed that the best time to start was after most Graham citizens had gone to bed, and to meet at the jail at eight o'clock.

Johnson also met with County Attorney Martin. Martin said, "It was the first intimation I had that the prisoners were to be taken away. Johnson called my attention to the fact that I had to be in Dallas the next week on a court matter and asked me to go along. We talked about how to move the prisoners . . . thought best to start about moonrise, so we would have light. He told me to secure a three-seated hack from Horton's livery, but not to let Horton know where or when we were going. I told Horton I had to go out in the country and wanted the best team he had. . . . Johnson told me who his guards were. He mentioned Logan, that he had wanted to go, or something of the kind. I spoke to Logan about it afterwards . . . asked if he was going. He said he had some sick folks at Belknap and they could not get along without him."[11]

By day's end, the matter had reached the ears of many and new trouble was brewing — as witnessed by J. T. Lovejoy: "January 19 was the last day for paying taxes without a penalty. I went to the sheriff's office [where John Levell had his desk as a collector], and found quite a crowd there — ten or fifteen, maybe eighteen men. . . . I knew Levell, Holman and Frank Harmison. The crowd was talking in a general way and pretty well filled with whiskey, from the appearance of things. I stepped up to pay my taxes, asked who was the man that had paid for the whiskey, and Harmison said, 'You can have some if you want any — no trouble about that.' Levell looked over the tax rolls and wrote me a receipt. While I was still in the room with the crowd, a Mr. Finlay said to me — so low no one else heard it — 'You will hear something before morning.'"[12]

The Marlows, Clift and Burkhart learned of their transfer shortly before dark. Johnson came to the jail with Levell and told them:

"Boys, get ready fast. I have orders to take you to Weatherford tonight. Nobody knows about it except me and my guards."

Alf asked, "Who are your guards?"

Johnson named them, and Speer told Alf: "It's a mob either way, but you will probably stand a better chance outside than in here."

Johnson looked startled, and Levell growled: "Go ahead and get ready — quick." They examined the Marlows' shackles, then fastened Clift and Burkhart together in a like manner.

Clift had difficulty getting his boot over his leg iron, so he tore off the top. "Here, Levell," he said, "I will give you this to remember me by."

"All right," said Levell, "I'll take it, for you will soon be in the pauper's field."

Clift asked what he meant, and Levell replied: "Oh, nothing — they will take you to Fort Smith, where they will probably hang you, and I won't see you anymore."

The prisoners hobbled downstairs. There were "ten or fifteen men on the ground floor," and Charles accused Johnson, "You lied to us, Ed." When the prisoners were ushered outside, "there were twenty-five or thirty more men standing around two hacks and a buggy," and they "could not tell the guards from anyone else." Charles pursued his concern, "Ed, you are taking us out to have us mobbed again," and Johnson assured him, "Nobody will run on us with my guard." Charles asked, "If they do, will you give us the guns?" and Johnson said, "Yes — and die with you if it comes to that."[13]

All six prisoners were placed in the hack obtained from Horton's livery — Charles and Alf on the rear seat, George and Epp on the middle seat, and Clift and Burkhart on the front seat with County Attorney Martin, as driver.

Johnson asked Martin if he was armed. Martin told him, "I have a small pistol in my pocket," and he said, 'Give it to me,' as it would not be prudent to carry a pistol in the hack, as the prisoners might overpower me."[14]

Criswell thought the prisoners should be better secured, and suggested: "What say we run a rope through their irons and fasten them to the back?"

Johnson shook his head. "Not necessary," he said.

Charles Marlow thanked him.[15]

Johnson then climbed into the front seat of the second hack beside Criswell. The back seat was occupied by John B. Girand and Marion Wallace. This hack contained extra Winchester rifles and a supply of ammunition. Sam Waggoner and Will Hollis took the buggy, and the three vehicles, thus filled and in that order, started for Weatherford at eight o'clock — a little before moonrise.

Above, a poster for The Sons of Katie Elder — *based on the exploits of the Marlow brothers — produced in 1965 by Paramount Pictures. Also from the film, the still below shows the brothers being shackled together.*

Blood Bath at Dry Creek

Martin drove swiftly away and soon was far ahead of the other vehicles. Knowing he had been with the mob on January 17, the prisoners grew uneasy.

George Marlow said: "You had better slow down, the guards are not coming."

"They'll catch up pretty soon," Martin grunted.

The night was very cold, and Clift asked if he did not want some more blanket over his lap.

"I do not want it in my way," replied Martin.

Taking in these suspicious points, Charles told the other prisoners: "We will be mobbed in fifteen minutes."

At this remark, Martin slowed the team. The guard hack and buggy came in sight, and the procession moved along the road together until it reached Dry Creek, two miles out of Graham.

Dry Creek was an intermittent stream rising six miles east of Graham and flowing southwest about seven miles to drain into Salt Creek. On the opposite side of the stream the road rose steeply between two pastures. The land on the left was cultivated excepting a large clump of scrub oak the height of a man's head inside the fence, about a hundred yards beyond the creek bed. The land on the right was covered with timber and underbrush, with an entrance gate near the top of the hill.

Before reaching the creek, the guard hack swung alongside, and Johnson hallooed Martin to stop. Johnson alighted, drew a flask from his coat pocket, handed it up to Martin, and said: "Maybe the boys need something to warm them up."

Martin took a swallow, then passed the flask to George Marlow. "Boys, have a drink!" he shouted.

The flask went around, the prisoners taking a little in their mouths but instantly spurting it out at Charles' whispered warning: "That shout was a signal. . . ."

The hack moved on, crossed the creek and started up the hill. The guard hack reached the opposite bank. The buggy was still in the stream bed. Charles Marlow, surveying the brush and timber in the moonlight, nudged his brothers.

"Get ready, boys. This is where they intend to kill us."

The words scarcely left his lips when a figure with a leveled rifle arose from the scrub brush on the left of the trail, and commanded "Halt! Hold up your hands!"

Martin jumped off the right side of the hack, ran to the head of the team, and yelled: "Here they are — take all six of the sons-of-bitches!"[1]

A crowd of masked men sprang from the brush, yelling and firing rifles and six-shooters, and rushed the prisoners and guards.

The first salvo riddled the front top of the guard hack above Johnson's head. One bullet ripped through the lapel of his overcoat, another through the brim of his hat. Seeing the badly excited Sam Criswell leap off the seat beside him and Girand and Wallace leave the vehicle and run, Johnson realized he had been double-crossed and drew his six-shooter to face the mob. At the same moment, someone sent a bullet tearing into his only hand, disabling him. The deputy marshal managed to cling to the weapon however, shouting for the Marlows to fight for their lives.

The Marlows already were in action. Martin had left the head of the team, running toward the timber. Charles and Alf leaped off the side of the hack away from the mob and hobbled as fast as their chains would permit to the guard hack and its supply of arms and ammunition. A man dashed up behind Johnson, grabbed the revolver from his hand, and was trying to pull him from the seat. Alf grabbed the man's Winchester; Charles wrenched Johnson's revolver from the man's hand and shoved it into his groin.

"Don't shoot," begged the man. "I am a guard."

"Let loose then," demanded Charles, and the man fled.

Simultaneously, George and Epp toppled over the side of the hack and hobbled to the scene. Johnson's frightened team ran up the creek bank with the guard vehicle and became entangled in the fence. Criswell dashed past George and Epp. They jumped on his back and bore him to the ground. George seized Criswell's Winchester; Epp took his revolver. Criswell ran toward the mob, and died twenty feet away, a bullet in his neck. Johnson, his hand bleeding badly, made his way down the road to the shelter of the creek bottom.

The mob formed a semi-circle and fired a volley upon the four Marlows — now armed, left to their own fate, and standing two together, back to back. The bloody battle at Dry Creek began in earnest.

The Marlows killed one of the mob leaders, Bruce Wheeler. According to the *Graham Leader*, "another man, shot in the arm, jumped up and down in the road, cursing like a pirate. . . . The others became demoralized [beat a hasty retreat into the timber on the right side of the road], and the prisoners held the field."

Burkhart had no stomach for the fight, but Clift, who

feared nothing, wrestled him from the hack. Pulling him on their chain, Clift tried to reach a rifle Bruce Wheeler had dropped in the road, and was shot in the left thigh. Burkhart dragged him back to the hack, and seized the reins of the lunging horses.

Charles and Alf were shooting to the left, George and Epp to the right. Three masked men passed close to Alf and fired several times pointblank. Alf reeled in agony. He threw down his empty revolver, snatched up a Winchester to fire back, but fell headlong, dead from fifteen bullets in his head, shoulders and chest.

George was hit in the right hand, the ball knocking his Winchester against his solar plexus with the such force that he was paralyzed for a moment. Epp fell at his side. George asked Epp if he could get up, and Epp said, "No — I can never get up anymore." He, too, had been shot to pieces and was bleeding to death.

George rested his rifle across his right arm, and working the lever with his left hand, poured shots into the mob until, shouting and cursing and leaving a trail of blood, they again fell back to the underbrush and trees.

Charles and George stood anchored to their dead brothers, Charles facing south and west, George south and east, their backs together. George sighted some men by the buggy in the bed of the creek, hardly discernible in the shadows, and said, "There are some of the bastards." He pointed his rifle, but Charles said, "Don't shoot down there, they are the guards."

George shifted his aim to fire into the brush. At the same instant, a shotgun roared from the creek. Charles sank to the ground with buckshot in the side of his head and chest. George fired at the buggy as it quickly disappeared down the bed of the stream.

George tried to get Charles on his feet. Charles struggled upward, but fell back, half sitting and half reclining on the body of Alf and gasping for breath.

George stood alone now. Still he did not lose courage. In a

frenzy of anguish and pain, he shouted to the attackers: "Come again, you cowardly bastards! We have plenty of ammunition, and nobody hurt. Come on!"

One man responded to his challenge — Frank Harmison, considered one of the gamest men in Young County. Harmison had been wounded as the mob retreated, but he was no quitter.

"Where are you going?" a mob member yelled.

"Back to see it out," Harmison replied scornfully and stepped quickly into the road.

George saw him coming, dropped his empty rifle and picked up Epp's revolver. The two men faced each other a moment in silence, then blazed away simultaneously. Harmison fell with a bullet between his eyes.

Busy with Harmison, George failed to see a tall figure slipping along the fence on the right side of the road, raising a pistol to shoot him. Charles, however, fired three times, hitting the man in the hip and side. He dropped his gun and sank down, but had strength enough to crawl away into the edge of the brush. Charles recognized his humped form and slate-colored slicker, and knew it was Eugene Logan.

With Logan out of the fight and Criswell, Wheeler and Harmison dead in the road, the rest of the mob no longer chose to face guns in the hands of desperate men and scattered to their homes and hiding places before daylight disclosed their identity to the law-abiding citizens of Graham. The guards had vanished. The battle at Dry Creek was over.

George knelt beside Charles, grasped him by the hand, and said, "Our brothers are dead and their souls are in Heaven."

"Yes," Charles responded, huskily. "Now we must get loose from them and out of here. See if you can find a knife in one of the dead men's pockets."

George dragged Epp to the body of Criswell, found a big clasp knife and dragged Epp back to Charles and Alf. George's hand was too badly injured for use, and he gave the knife to Charles. Charles whetted the blade on a large stone at the roadside, then carefully disjointed Alf's foot at the ankle and slipped off the leg iron. He then performed the same crude amputation on Epp, freeing George.

George gathered sufficient arms and ammunition from the field of battle, then helped Charles into the hack where Clift and Burkhart labored with the frightened team. Clift and Burkhart took the front seat.

Burkhart was shaking like a leaf. Clift's leg wound was painful, but he could still handle a gun. George handed him a six-shooter, and said, "Use it if necessary." Charles seemed close to death; the only available help was at the Marlow home. George ordered Burkhart, "Drive for your life!" and Burkhart whipped the team down the road in the moonlight.

George described their twenty-five-mile flight to the Denson farm:

We stopped at a house close to Finis [a little village in southwestern Jack County], as Clift and Charley wanted water. The man who came out refused our request and closed his door. We went on to Finis, hallooed there, but could get nobody out. There was a woodpile close by, and we got an ax and chopped the chain loose from Burkhart and Clift. Burkhart said he could not do anything chained, but as soon as he got loose, he ran into the brush, and that was the last we saw of him. We went past Finis to another house where nobody lived. Charley was feeling mighty bad . . . could not get his breath unless we would take his arms and hold them stretched out. We took him in the house, and he just fell over. I said, "Charley, are you going to give up?" He didn't say anything, then I kinder jerked him, and he said, "No," and commenced vomiting. After coughing up some clotted blood, he got better, and we started on home. We stopped at Denson's first and woke him up. He told us to go on down to our house and he would be there soon. . . .[2]

Home was reached in the cold gray dawn of Sunday, January 20. The agonized Marlow women were informed that Alf and Epp were dead, but there was no time to mourn. The house was converted into a hospital and fortified for the attack that the Marlows knew would come.

VIII

Siege at the Denson Farm

News of the Dry Creek fight was carried by young John Girand the two miles to Graham, which he made in about twenty minutes on foot. He reported that Johnson, half the guards, and all the prisoners had been killed. He probably believed it from the number of the shots he heard as he fled in the night.

Johnson, Marion Wallace, Sam Waggoner and Will Hollis soon arrived in town, however. Johnson was very weak from loss of blood. He was taken to his home, where physicians announced that his only hand was permanently injured, and his only explanation for his miraculous escape was that evidently his time had not come.

Wallace told how he had jumped from the guard hack when a ball went so close to his nose he could smell it. He threw his revolver in the face of the man who fired it, then ran about seventy-five yards and lay down until the prisoners hack drove away.

Hollis told Joe and Lizzie White at the Bell Hotel: "I stopped the buggy in the creek upon seeing my friends being shot down, but was prevented from firing on the mob by two men who came up on each side of the buggy. It was very hard not to be allowed to help my friends. I do not believe there is any God, or He would not allow good men to be killed that way."[1]

Again a report spread that an Indian Territory gang led by Boone Marlow had attacked the guards and rescued his brothers. This time the story apparently was contrived to arouse the people to demand vengeance. It lost steam, however, when Logan was discovered at the Woods House, shot in the hip and side, and a score of citizens led to the battle scene by Marion Wallace and a farmer named James Duty found the bodies of Criswell, Wheeler, Harmison, and Alf and Epp Marlow.

Duty conducted an extensive investigation; Lasater stayed only a few minutes. Lasater "did not see Logan at the Woods House, but talked to Will Hollis and Hollis said Logan was not a guard." Lasater "heard the same in Collier's presence during the night, and also heard it four or five times the next day."[2]

The irritated Sheriff Collier dispatched riders to different parts of Young County, asking as many people who could, and as soon as possible, to come to Graham to organize for the capture of the surviving prisoners.

Perry Harmison was informed by Marion Wallace that his son Frank was one of the guards attacked and slain by the mob. He reached Graham at daybreak, "highly indignant at the manner of his son's death," and announced "publicly and repeatedly" that he would give $10,000 for the capture of Frank's killers. He "kept thinking and talking that way" until Edwin S. Graham told him Frank was not a guard.[3]

Before the sun was an hour high, Sheriff Collier's avenging cavalcade began its march on the Denson farm. The cry now was: "Extermination of the Marlows — men, women and children!"

Disgusted with the state of affairs, Marion Lasater dispatched a message to Charley Auburg, who lived in Jack County below Finis. Auburg recently had been commissioned as a Texas Ranger by Governor Sul Ross. Lasater asked Auburg to meet him at the Denson farm at once.

Meanwhile, Marion Wallace rode to Jacksboro to solicit the help of Sheriff Moore. According to Moore, "he came to my house before daylight . . . told me the Marlows had got away again and wanted me to assist in catching them. He inferred that the mob were friends of the Marlows, that all the men killed except the two Marlows were guards, and I was under that impression when I set out gathering a posse from one side of the road or the other. I reached the Marlow cabin with twenty-five or thirty men about noon, and found Tom Collier with at least twice as large a posse gathered from Young County. . . ."[4]

Collier had demanded the surrender of the Marlows, which they rejected. They refused admission to anyone except a doctor. The women took up rifles with George and Clift and thrust the muzzles through the chinks in the sides of the cabin, presenting a solid front while they listened to the posse's loud debate as to the family's fate.

Sheriff Moore continued: "You could hear someone suggesting something every minute. I saw Verna Wilkerson, Waggoner and Levell there . . . knew Wilkerson, but was not very well acquainted with Waggoner and Levell. My men were tolerably 'hot' when we first got there, as all were thinking that Wheeler and Harmison were guards and that Boone Marlow's friends had killed them. . . . Collier wanted to load a wagon with hay and push it up to the cabin so they could go in there. Someone suggested burning the house or shooting it all to pieces."[5]

Marion Lasater arrived in the midst of the debate with Ranger Auburg and Dr. R. N. Price, of Graham. Lasater promptly took issue with Sheriff Collier and made the first attempt at a public speech in his life:

Men, there has been enough blood shed over this affair. Collier and his deputies have not brought you here in the interests of peace and justice, but as another mob bent on wreaking vengeance upon the Marlows, who have done nothing but defend their lives when attacked. I'm tired of this. I'm going down to that cabin and I'm going inside, if they will allow me, and if they will not surrender to me, at least see how they are. If the cabin is attacked while I'm in there, you will have to kill me before you get the Marlows. Come on, Doc [turning to Price], you are going with me.[6]

Lasater and Price strode down the hill, hands extended as tokens of their peace mission. The door opened and closed behind them as the posse watched with surprise and uncertainty. Lasater had never lied to the Marlows about anything and assured Martha Marlow that he would see that the doctor did only what was right. Doctor Price dressed Clift's and George's wounds, then examined Charles. "I can do nothing without putting you under an anaesthetic," he said.

"But I don't want to be put to sleep," Charles protested. "That mob might hit us at any moment."

George cocked his revolver. "Charley, let him put you to sleep, and if he don't wake you up when I think he ought to, I'll shoot him."

Doctor Price unceremoniously closed his pill bag. He stated that the buckshot should come out, but he did not consider the wounds fatal if treated soon and properly.

Lasater asked George if they would surrender and go with him and Auberg to Jack County. Again the brothers refused but declared their willingness to surrender to Marshal Cabell or his chief deputy, Captain W. F. Morton, at Dallas.

Lasater wrote the message, handed it to Doctor Price, and told him to dispatch it as soon as possible. "I'm staying here and will help fight the Collier crowd if I have to."

In the meantime, Sheriff Moore informed Collier that he

could not support an attack as the Marlows were United States prisoners: "I did not think we had any right to arrest them without a writ or warrant. . . . I decided to get Denson and go down to the cabin. James Duty said he would go with me. . . . When we got a little piece from Denson's house, Mr. Duty told me it was a mob of Young County men that had attacked the prisoners at Dry Creek. That was my first understanding of the affair. . . . Doctor Price came out of the cabin about that time with a message for Marshal Cabell. He asked if I would send it to Dallas; I told him I would. I went back to Collier and told him I would leave the matter alone. This made him very angry. He said it was a damned shame to let three men back off seventy-five, and intimated that it was cowardly to go off and not take them. I told my men to mount their horses, that if the Marlows would surrender to us, we would protect them, but since they refused to do so, we had no business there. I went back to Jacksboro and telegraphed Marhsal Cabell."[7]

Ranger Auburg stayed at the Denson farm two days: "Shortly after Sheriff Moore and his men left, I had a run-in with Marion Wallace. . . . Wallace was sorter north from Denson's house, about 300 yards from the cabin, and still anxious to take the Marlows out. I told him they were safe enough; that Lasater was with them, and they had agreed to go with the Marshal as soon as the Marshal could get there. . . . Collier stepped up and said something to Wallace, and Wallace said, 'I don't give a damn — the Marlows killed my uncle and I am going to have revenge.' He was going to take them out anyway, and I told him, 'I have the authority to forbid it . . . you will have to go over my dead body.' He sorter quieted down then, and I saw he was not going. . . ."[8]

Lasater remained in the cabin until five o'clock Monday evening, January 21: "The Marshal had not got there yet. I had word before I left town Sunday that my brother was lying at the point of death and was aiming to start down to see him Monday. He lives in Jack County. I drove the hack the prisoners had come in from the Denson farm back to Graham, and went direct from there to my brother's."[9]

George Marlow picked up the story: "We sent a message to Graham with the hack for our brothers' bodies to be sent down to Denson's. [The bodies of Criswell, Wheeler, and Harmison had been released to relatives; Alf and Epp had been placed on display side by side in the courthouse hallway where the public could view their disjointed ankles and the rock used to sharpen the knife]. Alf and Epp were brought in the evening, so shot to pieces that it was necessary to bind strips of cloth about them till they could be dressed for the grave. It was heart-rendering to look upon the sorrowing wife of Alf and my mother frantically kissing and talking to the two still forms. . . . At mother's request, Alf and Epp were buried in the Finis cemetery a few miles away. Quite a number of Jack and Young county men, at last getting their eyes open to the wrong done us, volunteered their assistance. Charley and I did not attend the funeral. We stayed in the house with our wives and Clift and kept our arms trained on Collier's guards. We could see men up south of the house, and up on the hill around Denson's place. Finally, Captain Morton came after us. . . ."[10]

Captain Morton was in Marshal Cabell's office when the telegram was received at Dallas, Monday morning, January 21: "Cabell ordered me to go to Weatherford that night and call on Captain Sisk and get him to go with me if he could. I reached Weatherford on the Texas and Pacific railroad about eleven o'clock; Sisk could not go, but got three men for me. After dinner I secured a conveyance and proceeded up the Graham road until I got to Finis, where I met Charley Auburg. . . ."[11]

Auburg had been notified of Morton's departure from Weatherford: "I wanted to get him to the Denson place as soon as possible and went to Finis and laid there until two o'clock Tuesday morning, as I was afraid I would miss him. I got him to the Denson place about 6:00 A.M. P. A. Martin,

Dink Allen and some others were in the woods, I suppose to keep the Marlows cornered. . . ."[12]

Captain Morton continued: "They stopped me and my men and asked who we were, and I told them. They had a little fire going under some mesquite trees. I asked who was in charge, and they said 'Collier, the sheriff.' I told them I wanted to see Collier. . . . Collier met me at the gate about daylight. I told him I had come for the Marlow boys and Clift by some orders of Marshal Cabell, and I wanted him to take his men away. He objected, saying the people would censure him for not being able to arrest them, and wanted four or five of his men to help me. I said, 'Mr. Collier, the people of Young County will approve your course in preventing more bloodshed, so take your men away,' and he promised to do this. I left my guard near the little house and went right in. I said, 'Boys, I have come for you, give me your guns.' George asked if I could protect them, and I told him I would. I fixed Charley a place to lie down in the hack and placed Clift in a position to hold up Charley so he could breathe. We left in fifteen or twenty minutes. Some of Collier's men were standing by the gate . . . horses hitched at the fence. Auburg and my guard were armed with Winchesters and six-shooters and I told them to go on with the prisoners. I gave Collier's men the guns the prisoners had carried away from the battle field . . . then drove toward the Weatherford road, and nobody followed."[13]

About a mile from the Denson farm, a young man galloped up behind Morton and asked where he meant to reach the railroad.

"Weatherford," Morton replied.

"You will be in the night, won't you?"

"Yes, right smart in the night."

The youth turned back at a lope.

Morton suspected a plot for another attack: "As a precautionary measure, I left the Weatherford road a few miles farther on and took the road leading to Palo Pinto. I reached

Palo Pinto Tuesday night, my guard and the prisoners all sleeping in the county jail. I telephoned Marshal Cabell the circumstance and that I would take the prisoners fifteen miles further south to Gordon, then to Weatherford. He told me to take the train at Gordon and bring them to Dallas."[14]

Morton and party reached Dallas on Wednesday night. Next morning, a government physician treated the prisoners' wounds. En route to Palo Pinto, Charles had coughed up one of the buckshot, and had coughed up another before boarding the train at Gordon. This natural expulsion of some of the lead so improved his breathing that the physician predicted a quick recovery.

Captain Morton told a reporter Thursday evening: "The prisoners have plenty of grit. They bore their wounds in silence throughout the journey, and were glad to get here safely."[15]

That night, Boone Marlow was slain on Hell Roaring Creek in the Comanche reservation, twenty miles east of Fort Sill. Word did not reach Dallas until January 28, when Sheriff G. Cooper Wright at Henrietta, Texas, telegraphed Marshal Cabell that three men had just passed through his city with the body, en route to Graham. The telegram gave no further particulars. The next day, three men drove up under a large oak tree at the corner of the courthouse square in Graham. They gave their names as Martin Beavers, G. E. Harbolt and J. E. Direkson, said they lived in the Chickasaw Nation, and invited Sheriff Collier to "come see what we have in our hack." Rolled in a blanket lay the remains of Boone Marlow, with two bullet holes in the forehead. The weather was very cold, and notwithstanding that Boone had been dead five days, "the body was as lifelike as though life had just become extinct."[16]

Justice Sterrett conducted an examination. The men gave a swaggering account of how they had located the fugitive on Hell Roaring Creek by trailing a party who had been carrying food to him; he had refused to give up peaceably, and they

Hell Roaring Creek, near Fort Sill, where Boone Marlow was slain.

had killed him. The authorities were satisfied, and the men were paid $1,500 of the reward money. The State of Texas declined to pay the additional $200 reward, since it had been offered for arrest and conviction.

Beavers, Harbolt and Direkson failed to reckon with the possibility of an autopsy. The wives of Charles and George Marlow happened to be in Graham to pick up the personal effects of Alf and Epp. Marion Lasater sought them out upon the arrival of Boone's body, and the women determined to wait in town until allowed to take it home. They informed Lasater that Boone had a sweetheart in the Harbolt family; that after fleeing to Indian Territory, Boone had made his presence known to her, only venturing from hiding to see the girl and pick up food she would leave for him. When the corpse was first exposed to view, Lasater had noticed there was no blood to speak of and that the two bullet holes did not look like gunshot wounds inflicted on a live body. An examination by Doctor Price revealed that Boone had died of arsenic poisoning.[17]

The Harbolt girl was brought to Dallas. She admitted that her brother, afraid to attack Boone openly, had mixed poison in the food he knew she would deliver to him. To share in the reward, Beavers and Direkson had retrieved the body and put two bullets in the forehead to make it appear Boone had been killed in a fair fight.

United States Attorney Pearre ruled it was illegal to poison a man even though he was a fugitive from justice, and charged the trio with murder. On March 28, they were released on $5,000 bail, and allowed to return home.[18] A few months later, Harbolt was shot to death in an altercation in the Chickasaw Nation; at the October term of the federal district court at Graham, Beavers and Direkson were given fifteen-year sentences.[19]

Boone Marlow was buried beside Alf and Epp at Finis — in one grave, enclosed by a stone wall, with a single headstone giving their names, ages, time and cause of death.[20]

IX

Indictments and Acquittals

The *Graham Leader* of January 24 labeled the Dry Creek ambush "the most disgraceful affair ever known in this country," and added, "The law-abiding citizens of Young County demand that proper authorities use every means to bring these violators to trial."

This the federal officials set out to do. Marshal Cabell sent Captain Morton and Deputy Marshal Ferd Tucker to Graham; U. S. Attorney Pearre sent investigator Lon Burrison to Belknap. Burrison took up residence at the Lauderdale House, famous for its gossip as well as its food. His probing aroused the citizenry to personal accusation, heated arguments and never-ending denials. The officers had only to separate the wheat from the chaff.

A. B. Gant dropped by John Levell's office on January 21 following the Dry Creek fight: "I made some remark about it,

87

and Levell said all he regretted about it was that they did not kill every one of the Marlows."[1]

Dixie Criswell had a conversation with Logan at the Woods House in reference to the death of her husband: "Logan said it was either Alf or Epp who killed Sam. Said the Dry Creek fight was a bad job; that if Johnson had tied the prisoners in the hack as Sam had wanted him to do, nobody would have been hurt but the Marlows."[2] In conversation with Mrs. Lauderdale, Logan was "not certain" who killed Criswell, but "thought George Marlow shot him in the back. . . . Said he had ridden ahead as an advance guard," was a hundred yards or two beyond where the mob appeared, and "rode back after the firing began."[3]

Clift and George and Charles Marlow refuted this — they had seen no horsemen in advance of their hack, nor anyone ride up after they were halted by the mob. Martin "did not see Logan until I found him wounded in the pasture and helped bring him to town."[4] And during the siege at the Denson farm, O. G. Denson "heard Collier say Logan was with the mob and could not get out of it unless he died out of it . . . he had the marks of it on him."[5]

Further evidence of Logan's connection was provided by James Duty and livery stable operators in Graham. Criswell kept his brown horse at the Broiles and Kramer stable. Late Saturday evening, January 19, Criswell had instructed both men to let Logan have his horse "if Logan called for it." Shortly after dark, Logan, in company with Bee Williams, "called for Criswell's horse, Williams called for his, and they rode off together."[6] Upon arriving at the battle scene, Duty "saw three horses hitched inside the south pasture, about seventy-five yards east of the gate . . . a brown horse I knew to be Criswell's, Bruce Wheeler's sorrel, and Frank Harmison's gray."[7]

Nor did Duty think County Attorney Martin's skirts were clean: "Martin was standing near the gate at the time. I was on the west side, Martin nearly in the gateway but nearer the east side, when a horseman passed between us. He bid Martin 'Good evening,' turned east on the Weatherford road and put his horse in a gallop. I asked who the man was, and Martin beckoned his head north, saying, 'A fellow who lives up country.' I asked him again, and he said it was Verna Wilkerson. Wilkerson lived north from Dry Creek.[8]

A few days after the fight, Les Randolph, a close friend of Sam Waggoner's, rode with the constable-deputy "from near Graham to Belknap. . . . Waggoner told me all about the mob at the jail on January 17, said he was there . . . told me all about the Dry Creek fight, and said it was good that Frank Harmison was killed, because he would have given the whole thing away."[9]

Lon Burrison arrested Waggoner and P. A. Martin. Captain Morton and Ferd Tucker took Logan into custody at the Woods House.

According to Morton, "Logan told me, 'This is hard to go as a guard of the prisoners and get wounded and then arrested for it.' Said when he rode back to the hacks . . . Charley Marlow commenced shooting at him; that he returned the fire until he shot away all his loads . . . was wounded and had to crawl off. . . . After arresting Logan, I had some talk about the trouble with Ed Johnson. Ed showed me his right hand, how it was shot. I said, 'Logan claims he was one of your guard,' and Ed remarked, 'I did summon him to go with me, but some of his family were sick. Logan was not one of my guard at all.'"[10]

Logan, Martin and Waggoner were taken before a federal grand jury at Dallas on January 25. James Duty, Marion Lasater, John Girand, Will Hollis, Dr. Price, John Levell and Marion Wallace were summoned as witnesses. The jury found indictment No. 456, substantially as follows:

That on the 19th day of January 1889 . . . Eugene Logan, P. A. Martin and Sam Waggoner, being persons of evil minds and dispositions, with Bruce Wheeler, since dead, and Frank Harmison, since dead — together with diverse other evil disposed persons whose names are as yet to the grand jurors unknown — did conspire, combine, and confederate and agree together to resist, obstruct and oppose one Ed Johnson . . . deputy marshal of the United States . . . in attempting to serve and execute certain four commitments issued by F. W. Girand, a commissioner of the United States for the Northern District of Texas. . . .

That George Marlow, Epp Marlow, Alf Marlow and Charles Marlow were duly and legally committed . . . and on said 19th day of January 1889, said Ed Johnson, in order to secure the safety and with a view to protect above United States prisoners from violence and death, did take into his custody and under his personal control and start with said prisoners to the city of Weatherford, in Parker County . . . and while still in Young County, Eugene Logan, P. A. Martin and Sam Waggoner, together with Bruce Wheeler and Frank Harmison, who were killed, and diverse other persons . . . names yet unknown . . . did go out upon the public road leading from Graham, Texas . . . and with shotguns and pistols and Winchester rifles attack while in custody of Ed Johnson above named prisoners and shoot and kill Alf Marlow and Epp Marlow, and wound George and Charles Marlow. . . ."[11]

The defendants were arraigned before U.S. Commissioner James Bentley at Dallas, ordered held on $2,500 bail each, and the case, styled *United States vs. Eugene Logan et al.*, No. 263, was transferred to the Graham court for prosecution. George and Charles Marlow, horse thievery cases still pending and in lieu of bail, were detained with Louis Clift at Dallas by Marshal Cabell, as government witnesses.

Captain Morton returned Logan, Martin and Waggoner to Graham on January 31. "In less than thirty minutes after their arrival, their bonds were made [before Commissioner Girand] and they were released."12

Federal court met at Graham on March 11, the Honorable A. P. McCormick presiding, United States Attorney Pearre for the prosecution, and Captain Morton acting in the absence of Marshal Cabell. Cabell had served as Democratic mayor of Dallas three times between 1874 and 1883, before his appointment as marshal by President Grover Cleveland, and had resigned to seek a fourth term as mayor prior to the March 4 inauguration of Republican Benjamin Harrison as the twenty-third president of the United States. "Graham is full of people. Hotels and boarding houses are crowded and numbers are encamped around town, having failed to get accommodation. This promises to be a very important term of court. . . ."13

A grand jury of twenty-three men were impaneled. Judge McCormick charged the jury as to the jurisdiction of the court in criminal matters in general, the duties of the jurors, and referred to the attack upon Johnson and his prisoners on January 19 as "the most serious offense ever committed in this District." He instructed the jurors to "carefully investigate this affair . . . present the guilty parties, however high they may stand in the country, officially or otherwise," and to "report any man to the Court who endeavors to talk to a juror on the subject or to influence his action in any way." In addition, he ordered Captain Morton to procure an "upper room" for the jury, saying it was impossible, in Graham, for them to conduct their deliberations on the lower floor of the courthouse and be safe from outside influences. James Duty was appointed bailiff, and the jury retired to nearby Beckham Hall to begin their labors.14

The civil docket was quickly disposed of and the criminal docket taken up on March 18. It consisted mostly of larceny and whiskey cases from Indian Territory. *United States vs. Henderson Brumley*, charged with conspiracy to rob the mail on the Texas and Pacific railway at Gordon, consumed two days, March 21 and 22, and resulted in acquittal. "The case was conducted before a great number of spectators"; however, the courthouse "could not hold the crowd that collected to hear the cases to come."[15]

Charles and George Marlow and Clift were brought from Dallas under strong guard. Charles' wounds had left him in such a weakened condition that at times he was unable to walk. George had the use of only his left hand. Clift was quite lame.

Indictments Nos. 235, 236 and 239 against Boone, Epp and Alf Marlow were dismissed by Judge McCormick on suggestion of their deaths by U. S. Attorney Pearre. George and Charles were tried for stealing the horses of Ba-Sinda-Bar. Witness Murphy, of Wilbarger County, declined to perjure himself to suit Deputy Johnson's interest, and excepting Ba-Sinda-Bar, the Indians endorsed on the commissioners complaints could not be located. In charging the petit jury, Judge McCormick commented that none of the horses and mules George had brought to Young County had been claimed as stolen and that, before their arrest by Johnson, none of the Marlows had ever been charged with crime or confined in jail.[16]

George and Charles were acquitted but continued in custody of the United States marshal in a new bail of $250 each until they could testify in the case of *United States vs. Eugene Logan et al.*[17]

Before being returned to Dallas, the Marlows and Clift testified before the grand jury. John Speer, who had been transferred to the Wise County jail at Decatur for safekeeping, was brought to Graham by deputy marshals for the same purpose. Judge McCormick certified the transfer of *United States vs. Eugene Logan et al.* to the Graham court, and by his own motion, set the case for trial at the October term.

O. G. Denson furnished bail for George and Charles Marlow, and on a promise to stay in Texas, they were at liberty — liberty, as George described it, "to stay in a section where men had connived to bring about our destruction and would resort to any means to destroy evidence or eliminate us as they had our brothers."[18]

George and Charles applied to the U. S. attorney for permission to carry guns, but their application was denied. They returned to Young County long enough to gather their womenfolk and moved to Gainesville, where they had "several old friends, and worked at anything they could get and as their health would permit."[19]

x

Brand of Infamy

In his March 4 inaugural address President Benjamin Harrison had stated in effect that the most hungry office hunters were not the most likely to receive favor with his administration. This was particularly true in the Northern District of Texas. On May 2, Captain George A. Knight, an ex-Union soldier from Gainesville and a dark horse candidate, was sworn in as United States marshal to succeed Cabell. In July, Eugene Marshall, a prominent Dallas lawyer, succeeded Charles Pearre as United States attorney; and J. H. Finks of Waco, heretofore district clerk at Dallas, became chief clerk for the district and circuit courts.

Not much of a politician, though always a Republican, Captain Knight had gone to Washington in mid-April, stating who and what he was and with about a dozen letters written by Democrats and Republicans alike endorsing his capacity,

95

character and standing in the Northern District. "Against the protest of the old machine," his two "favored" competitors were "knocked out unceremoniously," and his appointment "made the Texas gang bluer than ever."[1]

United States Attorney Eugene Marshall pursued the Young County mob case with vigor. At a special meeting of the Graham court in August, the grand jury returned two bills for felony. On August 12, Eugene Logan and P. A. Martin were arrested on new indictments charging them with complicity in the mob and the murder of Sam Criswell, Alf and Epp Marlow. The defendants promptly applied for writs of habeas corpus and gave bond — Logan in the sum of $7,500, and Martin, $5,000.[2]

Meanwhile, state district court convened at Graham, "Judge P. M. Stine presiding, W. B. Houston district attorney, A. T. Gay clerk, and Tom Collier sheriff all present. . . ." A state grand jury was impaneled, with J. E. Ryus as foreman. The civil docket was "run over on Monday and Tuesday [August 5 and 6] and the criminal docket taken up on Wednesday. . . ." In *State vs. Sam Burns*, Burns was found guilty and fined for saddle theft; in *State vs. John Speer*, Speer was acquitted and returned to federal custody. Defendants in five remaining cases won continuance or were released on bond. "This clears the jail of prisoners. . . . Court adjourned Thursday evening, August 15. Judge Stine and District Attorney Houston left for their respective homes on Friday morning. . . ."[3]

And a rumor swept Young County that the state grand jury had found a bill against Charles and George Marlow for the murder of Sheriff Wallace.

Eugene Marshall inquired of County Clerk Gay whether such a bill had been found. Gay refused to provide any information. Marshall discounted the rumor as having been circulated to frighten the Marlows from appearing as witnesses at the forthcoming term of federal court. Charles Marlow received a message at Gainesville from a friend in Graham, however, stating that the indictment did exist. The Marlows declined to answer the Young County indictment, convinced that Sheriff Collier and his deputies would not grant them proper protection.

On August 17, before state warrants could be sent to Cooke County, Charles and his mother crossed the Red River at Brown's Ferry, north of Gainesville. They then made their way across Indian Territory to Kiowa, Kansas, took a westerly course, and entered Colorado at Coolige. By month's end, they were at LaJunta. George and the other family members left Gainesville by rail, traveled through the Texas Panhandle and New Mexico, and rejoined Charles and Martha Marlow in Colorado. During the fall, Charles and George worked in the sawmills near LaJunta, making enough money to pay off their Texas bondsman. Then, with two mules and a heavily loaded wagon, they continued to Gunnison City and found work farther west, helping build a canal for conducting one of the icy mountain streams to the new town of Ridgway. In addition, they cared for a herd of cattle belonging to one Arthur Hyde, and thought they would have peace at last.[4]

Federal court met at Graham on Monday, October 21. Several civil cases were continued until next term. The criminal docket was taken up on Friday afternoon. When *United States vs. Eugene Logan et al.* was called, U.S. Attorney Marshall moved for continuance based principally upon the absence of key witnesses, Charles and George Marlow, and that a law-defying element had actually procured a state indictment of these witnesses for the purpose of preventing their appearance on behalf of the government. The motion was granted by Judge McCormick without argument.

The *Graham Leader* of October 31 asked:

> Is it possible that there exists in Young County such an element as this proposition suggests? We cannot learn whether the Marlows have been indicted or not, but if it is a fact that our last grand jury was prostituted for the

purpose of protecting or defending the mob who attacked the U. S. deputy marshal and killed two of his prisoners that night of January 19, then we tremble for the grand jury system. Sworn, charged with the rigid enforcement of the law, can it be possible that a lawless element made them their tools to do their biddings?

Editor John Conner of the *Fort Worth Evening Mail*, November 7, replied with an account of court matters at Graham obtained from Clerk J. H. Finks, whom he met on the train coming to Waco:

> Mr. Finks says the men who were indicted by the federal grand jury for murdering the two Marlows are making things exceedingly warm and unpleasant . . . have made dire threats toward the federal court, and at the recent setting it was found necessary to have eleven trusted deputy marshals in attendance. The court was compelled to disarm numbers of persons before entering the court room. Mr. Finks says that the last night spent in Graham the federal court officers, to guard against what they believed was an impending attack, slept in one room. Mr. Finks says the feeling there is so bitter that none of the cases mentioned can be safely tried at Graham and it will be necessary to have them sent either to Dallas or Waco. He says it will be a long time before the court at Graham will amount to anything again.

The *Leader* of November 14 took umbrage:

> The only truth in the statement is that Mr. Finks was in Graham during Federal Court. . . . He well knew the rest to be a falsehood throughout. We brand the whole thing an infamous in the extreme and stand ready to prove it, not for the sake of defending the Young County

mob, but . . . in the name of truth, decency, and in justice to the *good* people of Young County.

The *Fort Worth Mail, Gazette, Dallas News, Waco Day* and other exchanges are requested to copy.

Mr. Finks is especially requested to prove his allegations or swallow this brand of infamy.

The Finks statement appeared in most of the newspapers mentioned. The citizens of Weatherford held a meeting and "resoluted" about removing the federal court to the city, while the *Weatherford Sun* believed that sufficient prejudice existed in Graham and in Young County against federal authorities to render the argument justifiable.

The *Leader* of November 14 declared:

> The Weatherford cut against us is the most unkind cut of all. . . . The *Sun* editor manages to give publication to any rot he gets hold of or can extract from his diseased imagination to do the injury he says he don't want to do. . . . The claims of Weatherford to the Courts are unreasonable. In the first place she is not in this division of the district, and to put the Court there would require two acts of Congress. Then she is only sixty miles from Dallas and don't need a Federal Court. So it seems the *Sun* is taking a very unnecessary dish in a matter in which she is not liable to be concerned.

Again, on November 21, the *Leader* demanded that Clerk Finks answer his "accusation of falsehood. . . . He well knows that the people of Graham treated him and the other federal officers with all the courtesy and respect due them and their high authority. But he is as silent as an oyster on the subject. Upon evidence thus far presented we indict J. H. Finks as a libeler and slanderer of the first water, and ask him: 'What is your plea, guilty or not guilty?'"

Finks made his reply through a letter to U. S.

Commissioner Girand, published in the *Fort Worth Gazette*, November 28:

> I do not care to enter into a newspaper controversy, hence I write you, so that you may explain my position. In conversation with John Conner as to my trip to the Graham court, among other things talk of the mobbing of the prisoners came up. I said it was a bad state of affairs; that officers of the county were implicated; that we had a quiet term of court and very little business; that the marshal had several good and quiet deputies there in case of need; that no armed men were allowed to go in the court room while court was in session; that the United States attorney would move to have the case transferred to Waco or Dallas on account of prejudice at Graham; that Graham was an out-of-the-way place, sixty miles from a railroad, and it would be a long time before the court at Graham would amount to much — that is as to business; that on the night before we left Graham eleven of us, deputy marshals, etc., slept in one room and most of us on the floor, not that we feared an attack, but from necessity, on account of lack of accommodation.
>
> I am glad the *Leader* had no sympathy with the mob element, and I believe, while I have none with them, I have not done them injustice or stated anything but facts. I have no desire to do the people of Graham any injustice . . . yet it is my opinion that the attack on the prisoners has done Young County great injury by retarding its progress, which, I suppose will not be denied.

The *Leader* of November 28 commented:

> Although Mr. Finks did 'not care to enter into a newspaper controversy,' it seems he had got himself into one. We do not pretend to decide which is the correct version of the

Finks interview. We are certain, however, that there is a lie out, and it rests between *The Mail* and Mr. Finks. Let them decide the matter. Certain it is that someone could well profit by the experience of Ananias and Sapphire.

Eugene Marshall, in a lengthy report on the Graham trouble to Attorney General W. H. H. Miller in Washington, dropped this bombshell:

> The laws of the United States contemplate that the state will provide a suitable place for the use of the United States. The state, acting through its agency, the government of Young County, has failed to do this, but on the contrary its officers are in violent antagonism to the United States court . . . are charged with assaulting and murdering United States prisoners, and process of the courts of the state prostituted to shield from prosecution those who defy the law of the United States. I do not see how we can well avoid the necessity of armed men at Graham during sessions of the court to assist in the transaction of its business and preserve the peace. The atmosphere of shotguns and six-shooters is not a proper one for any court of the United States. It is to be hoped, therefore, that Congress will do something for the relief of this district by removing the branch of the federal court at Graham to some point more accessible to the public in these days of railways, and at which public business will not be embarrassed and obstructed by the lawless elements.[5]

The *Leader* called Marshall's report "a bloody shirt affair, gotten up for political purposes." The Washington correspondent for the *Dallas News* called on Attorney General Miller. Asked what plans he had for the Graham troubles, Miller "took a severe look of a man who intended to do his full duty or break a trace," and replied: "The United States marshal will receive instructions to secure the necessary number of deputies for the preservation of order." Did he have anything to say in regard to the removal of the court? "That is a matter with Congress," he said.[6]

At a November 30 meeting of Young County citizens, a committee was appointed to investigate Eugene Marshall. The committee charged Marshall had communicated with Congressman Silas Hare of Texas' 51st District to use his influence in moving the Graham court to Henrietta, center of the Fort Worth & Denver-Missouri and the Kansas & Texas railroads. Marshall contended his act was the privilege of a private citizen; the committee maintained that, as a commission for the president of the United States, his time should be spent looking into cases which it was his duty to prosecute. It further pointed to the fact that the indictments of Logan, Martin and Waggoner as principals in the murder of U.S. prisoners

> were found on the testimony of citizens of Young County. None of these witnesses have been molested. It is not proper that we should express any opinion as to the guilt or innocence of either of the parties indicted, as they are in the hands of the law, but we are free to say that they are entitled to a speedy and impartial trial, and we know that can be had [by jurors] from the counties which the court will order the jury drawn. We look upon mob law as an atrocious crime that should be severely punished, and if Marshall convicts any of the persons indicted, it must be done chiefly on the testimony of citizens of Young County. Then where is the prejudice in our county against the court?[7]

Judge McCormick let it be known that the court did not wish to borrow any "blood and nerve" for protection, stating in a letter published in the *Leader* on December 5:

I never have intended that any act or word of mine should be understood to mean that I desired the federal court, now held at Graham, to be removed from the place until the development of that division of the district should clearly indicate a more eligible place to hold the terms in that division. Now the Texas and Pacific railroad runs through five or six border counties on the south and the Fort Worth and Denver runs through three or four border counties on the north and through the very sparsely settled counties of the panhandle, while the body of that division, as to area and population, lies between these two roads, which are nearly 100 miles apart where they enter that division, and run further and further apart as they proceed. They connect only at Fort Worth, within a little over an hour's run of Dallas. Graham is ninety miles from Fort Worth and about eighty miles from Wichita Falls and Abilene, and the court is therefore about as centrally located now, with reference to the population and business of the settled portion of that division, as it could be. . . .

Judge McCormick's views quieted the controversy — temporarily.

A Furor of Legal Maneuvering

The removal controversy and the attack by the citizens committee on United States Attorney Marshall caused the government to shift the Young County mob troubles to the consideration of a grand jury in the U. S. Circuit Court for the Northern District of Texas, sitting at Dallas. In January 1890, the Dallas jury found four new indictments:

No. 492: That on the 19th day of January 1889, Eugene Logan, Bee Williams, Verna Wilkerson, Clint Rutherford, Frank Harmison and Bruce Wheeler . . . together with divers other evil disposed persons whose names are to the Grand Jurors unknown . . . did combine, conspire and confederate by and between themselves . . . to injure and oppress Charles Marlow in the free exercise of a right secured to him by the Constitution and Laws of the United States; to wit: the right to be protected by Ed Johnson, a deputy United States marshal. That Eugene Logan, in pursuance of and while in prosecution of said conspiracy . . . did assault Charles Marlow with deadly weapons . . . wound and maim him . . . while in the power, custody and control of Ed Johnson.

This indictment was filed February 11, 1890, as Case No. 33, *United States vs. Eugene Logan*.

No 493: Count 1 — That on the 19th day of January 1889, Charles, Epp, Alf and George Marlow, W. D. Burkhart and Louis Clift were citizens of the United States . . . in the power, custody and control of Ed Johnson, deputy United States marshal, by virtue of six separate writs, to wit: Warrants of Commitment issued by U.S. Commissioner F. W. Girand.

That Logan, Williams, Wilkerson, Rutherford, Harmison and Wheeler, together with divers other evil disposed person whose names to the Grand Jurors are unknown . . . did combine, conspire and confederate by and between themselves with force of arms to injure and oppress Charles, Epp, Alf and George Marlow, Burkhart and Clift in the free exercise and enjoyment of a right secured to them by the Constitution and Laws of the United States, to wit: the right to be protected from assault by Ed Johnson, deputy United States marshal.

That Logan, Williams, Wilkerson, Rutherford, Harmison and Wheeler, in pursuance of said combination and conspiracy . . . in the nighttime of said day . . . did go on the highway armed with shotguns, six-shooters and Winchester rifles, and did shoot off and discharge said deadly weapons to, at and against Charles, Epp, Alf and George Marlow, Burkhart and Clift while they were in the power, custody and control of Ed Johnson . . . did strike and penetrate Epp Marlow in the breast and side of the body . . . of which mortal wounds Epp Marlow did immediately die.

Count 2 — That Eugene Logan did shoot off to, at and against Alf Marlow a loaded gun . . . strike and penetrate the breast and side of the body of Alf Marlow, of which mortal wounds Alf Marlow did immediately die.

Count 3 — That Verna Wilkerson did strike and penetrate the body of Alf Marlow with leaden bullets . . . of which mortal wound Alf Marlow did immediately die.

Count 4 — That Clint Rutherford did shoot off to, at and against Alf Marlow a shotgun . . . loaded with buckshot . . . strike and penetrate Alf Marlow in the breast and side of the body . . . of which mortal wound Alf Marlow did immediately die.

This indictment was filed February 11, 1890, as Case No. 34, *United States vs Eugene Logan et al.*

No. 494: Counts were similar to those in 493, but added "did with those weapons kill and murder Epp Marlow" and that the prisoners were also "in custody of Thomas Collier, sheriff and jailer of Young County, under writs of commitment from the United States commissioner."

This indictment was filed February 11, 1890, as Case No. 35, *United States vs B. Williams et al.*

No. 495: Substantially the same as numbers 492 and 493, but adding John Levell and P. A. Martin as defendants, omitting the charge of murder and alleging a conspiracy to obstruct Deputy Marshal Johnson and Sheriff Collier in the execution of writs of commitment by "attempting to take George, Charles, Alf and Epp Marlow from the Young County jail on January 17."

This indictment was filed February 11, 1890, as Case No. 36, *United States vs. Eugene Logan et al.*[1]

The indictments against Logan, Martin and Waggoner by the grand juries at Dallas and Graham in January and August of 1889 contained charges similar to the counts in cases 33, 34, 35 and 36. By virtue of capiases or warrants issued by the Circuit Court, Logan, Williams, Wilkerson and Rutherford were arrested by Marshal George Knight, confined in the county jail at Dallas, and denied bail.

This set off a furor of legal maneuvering.

Sam Waggoner applied for witnesses to prove he was nine miles from Graham the night of January 17 when he allegedly attempted, with others, to "take the Marlows from jail for the purpose of killing them," and that he "did not request anyone [at Bryson] in Jack County to join in the mob." Bee Williams made a similar application to prove he was "at Belknap, twelve miles from the scene of the killings the night of January 19." Neither defendant "had sufficient means to pay the fees for such witnesses or the Marshal for service upon same," and asked that the witnesses be furnished them at government expense. Judge McCormick instructed Clerk Finks to "issue the process prayed for."[2]

Logan, Williams, Wilkerson, Rutherford and Levell, by their attorneys Robert Arnold and Robert Holman, moved to quash indictments 492, 493, and 495, because, first, they were found and presented by a grand jury at the United States court holding sessions in Dallas — offenses charged therein were committed in Young County and cognizable at the term of the district court at Graham; second, the indictments charged no offense against the laws of the United States — showed upon their face an offense against the laws of the State of Texas, of which the courts of that State had exclusive jurisdiction; third, the indictments were "bad" as no such right of George Marlow and others to be protected by a deputy United States marshal was secured by the constitution and laws of the United States, and the court, therefore, had no jurisdiction; fourth, there was no lawful penalty which could be imposed by the United States court for the offense of murder, if committed, as alleged, while defendants were carrying out, as alleged, a conspiracy to injure and oppress Charles Marlow and others — article 5509 of the Revised Statutes of the United States, which provided that any felony or misdemeanor committed in carrying out a conspiracy shall be punished by the laws of the State wherein committed, was inoperative since the penalties to be incurred varied with the laws of the several States of the Union and was, therefore, unequal in operations upon citizens throughout the several States in which the United States court exercised jurisdiction.[3]

In a separate application to the Circuit Court at Dallas, Logan, Williams, Wilkerson and Rutherford "ever prayed" that each be admitted bail until such time as they could be tried in due process of law.[4]

Defendants' motion to quash and the application for bail were denied.

At the March sitting of the Graham court, U. S. Attorney Marshall moved for continuance of the mob cases to the October term — again due to the absence of George and Charles Marlow. Judge McCormick granted the motion, and all witnesses summoned were discharged.

On application of the U.S. attorney, Judge McCormick commanded Marshal Knight to arrest George and Charles Marlow as "competent witnesses on the trial of cases Nos. 33, 34, 35 and 36" and "safely keep and have them before me to be dealt with according to the law." Knight returned the writs on March 27, "not executed, as after due diligence . . . defendants could not be found in the Northern District of Texas or Indian Territory."[5]

Word passed that the brothers had jumped bail, but bondsman O. G. Denson assured the government that he had been satisfied. In July, Marshal Knight inserted an advertisement in the *Dallas News* and the *Denver Times*, stating that the Marlows were wanted as witnesses in Texas and offering a $500 reward for their apprehension, or $250 for any news concerning them.

George and Charles had homesteaded some government land southwest of Ridgway, near Ouray, in Ouray County, Colorado. At Gunnison City, Sheriff Shores saw the reward offer in the *Denver Times* and, accompanied by two possemen named Bennett and Harper, made the trip across the mountains to the Marlow ranch. The officers arrived shortly before noon. George and Charles invited them into the house, but "sensing something was afoot," were "careful not to let the sheriff or either of his helpers get the drop on them."[6]

Shores stated his business frankly — he was there under his authority as deputy United States marshal for the district to arrest them and return them to Texas. The Marlows quietly informed him that they would not submit to arrest or under any circumstances lay down their arms; that they did not wish a recurrence of their experience in Young County. Martha Marlow announced dinner, and the men took their places at the table — George at the east end, Charles at his left on the south side, Shores and Bennett at the west end, and Harper on the north side.

The argument waxed warm. Shores reminded the Marlows that when a man was wanted by the United States as a witness, the government took means to get him. He insisted that they were foolish not to surrender.

In a tense moment, Shores dropped his fork on his plate. An exploding stick of dynamite would have produced no greater effect. In a split second George had the muzzle of his six-shooter against Shores' stomach; Charles had his hand on the butt of his revolver lest Bennett and Harper made a move.

Shores said: "You boys are taking things wrong, making a bad mistake."

He proposed that they go with him to Gunnison City, where he would swear them in as deputy sheriffs so they could carry guns. He would pay all their expenses and board them until Marshal Knight arrived from Dallas and arrangements could be made guaranteeing them safe conduct to Texas and back to Colorado. George and Charles accepted.

110

Marshal Knight reached Gunnison City three days later. His argument was the same as Shores had made at the Marlow ranch, but he agreed the brothers should take no further risks with the Young County mob element.

Knight "wanted to dress the boys for the trip." Consequently, George and Charles were "dolled up in silk shirts, narrow-brimmed felt hats, toothpick shoes shined to brilliance, light-colored trousers and coats, gray wigs, and their mustaches blacked." They "looked like an elderly pair of dudes — even our close friends would not have known us." Knight took the shortest route back to Texas. The Marlows went to Kansas City and from there took a southbound train to Dallas, where they met the marshal "at a point previously agreed upon."[7]

Marshal Knight made no explanation of why he had returned alone. His reputation was clear — when he located a man he wanted, he brought him in. His failure to do so this time and the manner in which he "averted questions" caused the accused conspirators to assume he had "killed the Marlows." Their rejoicing "subsided" when it was learned that the brothers had been shuttled from Dallas by rail and were under "proper protection" at Weatherford.[8]

Judge McCormick convened court at Graham on Monday, October 20, with Marshal Knight and Clerk Finks present; Eugene Marshall representing the pleas of the government, with Colonel William L. Crawford, ex-Confederate soldier and noted criminal lawyer of Dallas, employed as special district attorney to lead the prosecution of the mob cases; and Robert Arnold and Attorney Jerome C. Kearby of Dallas counsel for the defendants. Kearby had served with Colonel Charles de Morse's regiment of Texas Cavalry during the Civil War and as district attorney of the Palestine district under Governor Edmund J. Davis in 1872. Since 1880, he had been active in the Greenback party, the Union Labor party, the Anti-Monopoly party, and was among the first Populists in Texas.

Said the *Leader* of October 22:

grand jury of twenty-three men was impanneled. . . . Judge McCormick's charge was short and quite comprehensive, instructing the jury as to offenses within the jurisdiction of the U. S. courts and ferreting out crimes against the peace and dignity of Uncle Sam. . . . G. H. Crozier has accepted the position of crier and prays for the United States and these honorable courts twice a day. . . . Graham is full of strangers . . . large crowds of people from all parts of the country.

On October 29, the *Leader* reported:

The civil business of the court was disposed of Friday, Saturday and Monday [October 24, 25 and 27]. The criminal docket of the District Court was disposed of on Thursday [October 23]. Three old Indian Territory cases were tried and the defendants all came clear. The other cases were continued.

Eugene Marshall then moved that the several bills of indictment (mob cases) be tried together, because they "charged cognate and kindred crimes and presented parts and phases of the same transaction." The motion was granted and the indictments were combined "No. 34, Consolidated, *United States vs. Eugene Logan et al.* — Conspiracy to injure and oppress a citizen of the United States in the exercise of civil rights and murder of said citizen."[9]

Defendants moved to quash and dismiss this prosecution under the same objections made and denied in February. Judge McCormick overruled, and defendants excepted.[10] McCormick set the mob cases for October 30 and ordered a venire of sixty men to "appear forthwith."[11] The *Leader* continued:

Eugene Logan, Wm. Williams, Vernon [sic] Wilkerson and Clint Rutherford were arraigned yesterday. . . . They plead "not guilty. . . ."

112

Logan and Wilkerson seem quite well and hearty, despite their long confinement in prison [Dallas jail], but Williams is greatly emaciated and but a shadow of his former self. He had to be carried to and from court in a vehicle, as he is too weak to walk. . . . [Williams moved for a continuance of No. 34, Consolidated, as to himself, due to being confined in bed for three months under constant treatment of a physician and reduced to such condition that he was unable to endure the excitement of a trial in his cause].

The Marlow brothers are held at Weatherford until needed here. We suppose their coming will be attended by all the 'pomp and circumstance' of military espionage.

Marshal Knight and his deputies have been busy summoning special venire men.

There are [half a dozen] defendants indicted heretofore, others to the list before they adjourn. . . .

Shortly after noon, October 30, the foreman of the grand jury passed a bundle of documents to Judge McCormick and announced there was no further business before that body. The judge thanked the jurors for their patient attendance, and discharged them. In an *Extra* issue of Friday, October 31, the *Leader* reported:

The documents soon proved the jury had been at work. In a short time deputy marshals were scouring the town with warrants for the men indicted. . . . David [Dink] Allen was the first corralled . . . then followed the arrests of Robert Holman. T. B. Collier, Marion Wallace and John Levell, in quick succession. The deputies then got a fresh supply of warrants and brought in W. R. Benedict, E. W. Johnson, Pink Brooks, Dick Cook and Will Hollis. Late in the afternoon they arrested Jack Wilkins [a prominent Young County cattleman].

The prisoners were taken to the federal court and

113

placed under a strong guard. All were arrested under a charge of conspiracy to deprive citizens of their rights under the constitution and laws of the United States and murder in pursuance of the conspiracy.

The cases against Robert Holman, David Allen, E. W. Johnson and Will Hollis are all new and a great surprise to most people.

The Sheriff being under arrest, his duties are now performed by I. H. Carmichael, who was appointed deputy sheriff by Collier some days ago.

Excitement runs high and various opinions are expressed as to the course the authorities will now take.

U.S. Attorney Marshall promptly moved to set aside the former order of consolidation so far as to separate cases 33, 34, 35 and 36 and sever Levell and Martin from their co-defendants, leaving No. 34, Consolidated, to stand for trial against Logan, Williams, Wilkerson and Rutherford. McCormick made an order accordingly, except as to Bee Williams. Williams was jailed at Sherman and his cause continued due to his physical condition.

Defendants' attorneys made no exception but moved to quash the special venire, since Logan, Wilkerson and Rutherford were "charged with simple felonies under No. 34, Consolidated, and were therefore entitled to trial by regular jurors."[12]

Logan, Wilkerson and Rutherford then severally pleaded not guilty and applied for the testimony of the persons incarcerated at Graham — Allen, Holman, Collier, Wallace, Levell, Benedict, Johnson, Brooks, Cook, Hollis and Wilkins.[13]

XII

The Conspirators on Trial

The trial of Eugene Logan, Verna Wilkerson and Clint Rutherford began November 6, 1890. People from throughout the Northern District and elsewhere flocked to Graham by stagecoach, in wagons, buggies and on horseback. Families came in covered wagons and camped about the town for a week. Authority was given Marshal Knight by Washington for "swearing in all special deputies required to prevent rescue of the prisoners and to protect the chief witnesses and two surviving Marlows from attack." All persons entering the courthouse were searched for weapons, and an anteroom next to the door was "filled with six-shooters, bowie knives and rifles."[1]

Eugene Marshall and Colonel Crawford conducted a "most

able prosecution"; Kearby and Arnold "made a grand defense
— fighting every inch of the ground." More than 100 witnesses reiterated the statements and recollections set forth in
previous chapters of this work. Defense witnesses "recently
arrested" were confined to the county jail, except when called
to testify. Ed Johnson, "being quite ill," was allowed to
remain at home, under guard. Testimony taken by expert
stenographers from Dallas "filled a volume of closely typewrit-
ten pages."2

The most damaging testimony came from P. A. Martin,
who in effect became a witness for the prosecution.
Defendants' counsel claimed the right to examine Martin on
his *voir dire*, and handed him a transcript from the Superior
Court of Iredell County, North Carolina, showing the verdict
of the jury, the judgment of the court and sentence of Phelete
A. Martin for felonious homicide.

"I am the Phelete A. Martin spoken of in this transcript,"
Martin admitted. "I served out this sentence."

Defendants' counsel introduced the transcript in evidence and
objected to Martin testifying because he had been convicted of a
felony. Judge McCormick overruled the objection, counsel
excepted, and Colonel Crawford resumed the examination.

Martin summarized events leading to the Dry Creek fight,
then continued:

> As we got up the bank on the other side of the
> creek . . . where the road runs a little southeast towards
> Weatherford . . . we were halted by a mob of armed and
> disguised men. Part of the men came from the left side
> of the road, out of a clump of bushes next to the pasture.
> There was a pasture on the other side of the road. The
> parties that came from the left side began hollering,
> "Halt!" and "Hold up your hands!" They presented
> guns, and two of the party came directly in front of the
> horses. I dropped the lines. The horses went a little to
> one side and stopped. . . .

Despite the testimony of Charles and George Marlow and Louis Clift, Martin denied that he had shouted,

"Here they are — take all six of the sons-of-bitches!" and declared: "I never used such language in my life. I said, "For God's sake, fellows, don't shoot."

I jumped out of the right side of the hack and ran around in front of the horses . . . then dodged around on the left side where the first men came from. I ran northeast . . . further from the mob . . . to a clump of bushes across the road. I had gone about seventy-five yards when I met Marion Wallace. He was disarmed and had lost his hat.

Wallace and I went further up the fence and crossed the road into the other pasture. Just after I got into the pasture a man rode up to me and presented his gun . . . had a handkerchief over his nose. He asked who I was. I told him, and he galloped off east. . . .

I heard some parties out in the road a little distance from me . . . walked out there and spoke to them. They were Verna Wilkerson and Bee Williams. Williams had a dark cloth over his face. Wilkerson had his face blackened and was armed with a double-barreled shotgun . . . said he thought he got two of them [the Marlows]. I asked them who all were killed or hurt, and they asked me the same question. I told them I thought Bruce Wheeler was killed — that he was the man I saw fall off to my right. . . . Wilkerson told me that Clint Rutherford was wounded and thought Jack Wilkins was hurt too.

I saw ten or fourteen men out there I reckon. . . . I did not know what became of the Marlows . . . they got out of the hack some way. I heard them alternately praying, cursing and fighting . . . making more noise than any two men I ever heard . . . daring the mob to come back.

I think Frank Harmison returned after this. Verna

Wilkerson told me Harmison was wounded but had gone back again . . . said he tried to keep Harmison from going, but Harmison had gone back and they had killed him.

There were three or four horses hitched in the woods. Bee Williams rode off on one of the horses. He rode a black horse. I do not know what kind of horses Harmison and Criswell had. . . . After that, Mr. Logan came up from where the fight took place. He was staggering . . . I supported him a distance, and he fell on the ground and commenced begging for water. I had a little whiskey left in the bottle in my pocket, and he drank some of it. That seemed to revive him. . . . He told me he had received two wounds. He had on a slicker, but was not disguised in any way.

Wilkerson and I remained there with Logan until the prisoners left the hack. Then Wilkerson and I went down to inspect the battle field. I suggested that a crowd would be coming out from town pretty soon, and Wilkerson said he had better go down to the creek and wash the black off his face. I did not go to the creek with him . . . did not see him any more until he rode out of the pasture gate after several parties came out from town.

I saw Epp and Alf Marlow dead in the road . . . lying close together, their feet near each other, and one foot of each man cut off at the ankle. There was a Winchester and six-shooter at the side of Alf Marlow. I put the six-shooter in my pocket, because it was a large white-handled gun and I recognized it as being Ed Johnson's. I later gave it to Ed Johnson. Robert Holman came up with Tom Collier and two other men. Holman was carrying a shotgun. I gave him the Winchester. He was speaking about following the prisoners, and I told him they were well armed.

I did not go in search of the Marlows that night. We

put the dead bodies into a wagon to bring them in . . .
put Logan in a hack and brought him to town. I came in
a buggy with Sterrett, and went to the courthouse with
him and assisted in holding an inquest.

Martin also denied being present during the attack on the
jail the night of January 17:

"I went there afterwards. Logan told me the leader of the
mob was the tallest man he ever saw, and had a beard like a
horse's tail. Levell said the man had a gun that looked big
enough to crawl into. Criswell and Marion Wallace told me
they had been led to the graveyard with ropes. . . . They treated the matter as a very light occurrence . . . laughed about it."

Cross-examined by Kearby, Martin admitted being under
indictment for conspiracy in the attack and under bond. Had
he any agreement with the government by which this prosecution was to be discharged or dismissed?

Martin said, "I do not exactly understand it that way. I
have testified before the federal grand jury at Graham. I do
not know about being a willing witness, but since then I have
never tried to evade process of the court or keep from testifying. I have nothing against these defendants at all, and am not
a voluntary witness against them, but I realize the government cannot prosecute me and make a witness out of me at
the same time, if that is what you want to know."

Martin had continued to perform his duties as county
attorney. His term was about to expire, and he had written a
proclamation to the people of Young County, thanking them
for their kindness to him.

He concluded: "I am a very poor man . . . have no property at all subject to execution. I had trouble making my last
bond of $5,000. Mr. Arnold is on my bond, and he is defend-
ing these defendants."[3]

Prosecution and defense closed their arguments November
18. The jury reported November 22: "We, the jury, find the
defendant Clint Rutherford not guilty. The jury cannot agree

as to Eugene Logan and Verna Wilkerson." Judge McCormick discharged Rutherford from the indictment and entered a mistrial as to Logan and Wilkerson. Logan and Wilkerson moved for bail, which McCormick denied, then committed them to the custody of the U. S. marshal until the next term of court. Wilkerson was returned to Dallas. Logan was delivered to the custody of the Grayson County jailer, at Sherman, by Deputy Lon Burrison.[4]

The *Leader* of November 26 reported:

> The other parties who were indicted in the matter at this term applied for bail, and the Court, after hearing some evidence . . . decided that Robt. Holman, W. R. Benedict, Jack Wilkins, W. C. Hollis, Pink Brooks and Dink Allen were entitled in the sum of $5,000 each, which they immediately gave and were discharged from custody. . . . Defendants Tom Collier, John Levell, Sam Waggoner, Dick Cook, E. W. Johnson and Marion Wallace were remanded to the custody of the U. S. marshal until the next term. Marshal Knight left for Dallas on Sunday [November 23], taking the prisoners with him. They will be kept at either the Dallas or the Sherman jail.

Jail quarters at both Sherman and Dallas were limited, and Marshal Knight lodged his prisoners in the Tarrant County jail at Fort Worth.

The *Leader* bemoaned:

"It is a matter of deep regret that the jury failed to agree. The whole tedious trial will have to be gone through again. The expense of this term of court was enormous."

In a separate hearing before Judge McCormick on December 6, Marion Wallace was granted bail for eight weeks in the sum of $10,000. Physicians testified that a tumor on his neck of over a year's growth was "interfering with his respiration and would likely kill him if not removed by surgical operation," which they declined to perform in jail.[5]

By the end of November, Charles and George Marlow were back in Colorado with their families, convinced that had they not been under heavy protection by the government their blood would have soaked the Texas soil already made red by that of their brothers. Thirty-five special deputies sworn in during the court session, together with the field deputies that provided them safe passage to and from Young County, made a guard of fifty-two men in all.

The brothers "attached no blame to the jury — they were twelve men, tried and true. Their verdict was attributed not to the evidence or lack of it, but to the fact that they were afraid for their lives if they found the prisoners guilty."[6]

The bold stand taken by Marion Lasater against Collier and his posse at the Denson farm had done much to change public opinion in Young County. While the sober-thinking element applauded his action, the alleged conspirators and their followers condemned his sympathies for the Marlows. The question naturally entered politics and divided the people, regardless of party affiliations in national and state affairs. In the fall elections of 1890, two tickets were put in the field — the "mob" and "anti-mob" tickets, headed by Collier and Lasater, respectively. The campaign was one of intense excitement, the alleged conspirators and instigators of the mobs remaining in possession of the legal machinery until most of them were indicted and arrested. On November 4, before the trial of Logan, Wilkerson and Rutherford began, Marion Lasater was elected sheriff, and a young lawyer, J. W. Akin, succeeded Martin as county attorney.

XIII

Wounded Justice

In the Sherman jail, Bee Williams' health continued to deteriorate. Early in January 1891, he was transferred to the jail at Belknap to be cared for by family physicians; he died a week later. In mid-January, Tom Collier died of typhoid fever in the hospital ward of the Tarrant County jail at Fort Worth. His remains were embalmed by a local undertaker and shipped to the home of his parents in Alabama. A despondent Dick Cook was suffering from the same malady, but Fort Worth physicians announced that he would survive.

While Young County friends and relatives mourned the deaths of Williams and Collier, George and Charles Marlow returned to Dallas from Colorado for the March term of district court at Graham. At Dallas, they were issued the strangest documents in Texas history, worded as follows:

UNITED STATES OF AMERICA)
Northern District of Texas   )

Know all Men by These Presents, That I George A. Knight, U.S. Marshal, in and for the Northern District of Texas, do hereby constitute and appoint George Marlow of the County of Dallas, State of Texas, my true and lawful Special Deputy.

To hold Chas. Marlow in custody as an attached witness in the U. S. Court at Graham, Texas, I hereby authorize him to do and perform any and all things necessary to the execution of the process herein before enumerated and set forth as fully as I myself could do.

Witness my official signature this 27th day of January, 1891.

GEORGE A. KNIGHT
U.S.M.

I, George Marlow do solemnly swear that I will faithfully execute all lawful precepts directed to the Marshal of the Northern District of Texas, under the authority of the United States, which may come into my hands, and true return make; and in all things will truly, and without malice or partiality, perform the duties of the Marshal's Deputy of the Northern District of Texas, during my continuance in office and take only my lawful fees. And I do solemnly swear that I will support and defend the Constitution of the United States against all enemies, foreign and domestic; that I will bear true faith and allegiance to the same; that I take this obligation freely, without any mental reservation or purpose of evasion; and that I will well and faithfully discharge the duties of the office on which I am about to enter. So help me God.

GEORGE MARLOW

Subscribed and sworn to before me this 29th day of January A.D. 1891.

CHAS. H. LEDNUM,
U. S. Commissioner.

Special Deputy U.S. Marshals Charles and George Marlow at Graham during the conspiracy trial in 1891.

To the Hon. A. P. McCormick

U. S. District Judge

Sir: I, Chas. H. Lednum, do hereby certify that George Marlow Special Deputy United States Marshal, whose name appears to the oath above, did subscribe and was sworn to the same before me.

> CHAS. H. LEDNUM,
> U. S. Commissioner.

Charles' appointment and oath of office were identical except for the wording: "To hold George Marlow in custody as an attached witness in the U. S. Court at Graham, Texas."

Thus the two brothers became federal officers in the very section where they had been accused of every crime on the calendar and, as government witnesses, were *in custody of each other*.

U.S. Attorney Marshall arrived in Graham on Sunday morning, March 8. Marshal Knight and deputies, including Charles and George Marlow, arrived late in the evening with the prisoners from the Dallas and Fort Worth jails, and incarcerated them in the Young County jail in the care of Sheriff Marion Lasater. Judge McCormick convened court Monday morning, shortly after the arrival of Colonel Jerome Kearby to represent the defendants. The civil docket was called in the afternoon, but "none of the cases were tried." The United States attorney "dismissed about twenty old cases from the Indian Territory, which had been on the docket for a number of years. [These] dismissals were recommended by the Attorney General in Washington." [1]

Marshall then moved and Judge McCormick ordered to be added to No. 34, Consolidated, the indictments found by the grand jury in October 1890, charging Levell, Collier, Johnson, Wallace, Hollis, Cook and others with the same conspiracy as Logan, Waggoner and Wilkerson and, in pursuance thereof, the attempt to lynch on January 17 and the murders on January 19, 1889. On motion of the U. S. attorney, suggesting the deaths of Williams and Collier, the indictments as to them were dismissed.[2]

126

No. 34, Consolidated, *United States vs. Eugene Logan et al.* now included all the Young County mob cases.

Defendants excepted to the consolidation order. Levell, Logan and Waggoner moved to quash the indictments against them, and the other defendants excepted to the several indictments so consolidated on the same grounds stated in their motion to quash in October. Judge McCormick overruled both motions; defendants objected and pleaded not guilty.[3]

Logan and Wilkerson then filed a special plea that they had once been in jeopardy for the same offense — had been tried for the same conspiracy and murder by a jury at the October term; that "the jury was unable to agree as to these defendants," and the court, "on its own motion, and without consent of these defendants or either of them, discharged said jury from further consideration of this case." Marshall filed an exception in the nature of a demurrer; the court "held defendants' plea for naught" and sustained the exception.[4]

Finally, on motion of the U. S. attorney and by order of the court, Brooks, Benedict, Holman, Allen, Wilkins and P. A. Martin were severed from their co-defendants, leaving No. 34, Consolidated, to proceed against Logan, Wilkerson, Johnson, Levell, Wallace, Waggoner, Hollis and Cook.[5]

A special venire reported in court Thursday, March 26, and the government announced they were ready for trial. Copies of the indictment, endorsed with the names of witnesses upon whose testimony the indictment had been found, were delivered two days previous. However, no list of witnesses "to be produced at the trial for proving the indictment" had been delivered to any of the defendants. Defendants suggested these facts, and moved that they not be required to proceed until such lists should be furnished. McCormick overruled the motion, and defendants excepted.[6]

Friday morning, defendants announced they were ready for trial, "except Johnson, who is not physically able to attend, and the court allowed him to sever on that account." (The wound Johnson had received at Dry Creek was slow to heal;

127

his family had to feed him and put clothes on him. For nearly a year, he would remain almost helpless.)[7]

In impaneling the jury, Eugene Marshall put this question: "Have you any conscientious scruples in regard to infliction of the death penalty for crime?" Each juror who answered that he had such scruples was challenged for cause. The defendants objected, "because the jury in the United States court has nothing to do with the penalty, but passes upon guilt or innocence . . . and it is not one of the disqualifications of jury service under the laws of the United States." The court overruled these objections, and defendants excepted.[8]

Jury selection was completed Friday evening. On Saturday, the bills of indictment were read to defendants. All entered pleas of not guilty.

Witnesses were sworn on Monday, March 30, and instructed to "keep out of the courthouse, but within reach of the U. S. marshal, and not to talk about the case nor allow anyone to talk to them about it. . . . The government began taking testimony Monday evening. Stenographers employed by both sides recorded the evidence in full."[9]

During several trying and tedious days, George and Charles Marlow recapped their tribulations, as nearly as they were permitted under grueling cross- and re-cross-examination by Colonel Kearby and Robert Arnold. The government built its case around Eugene Logan as a mob leader, and when Charles stated he had told George, Clift and Burkhart that he believed Logan was the man he had shot at just before escaping in the hack following the Dry Creek fight, defendants objected to his evidence as declarations made in their absence, and as hearsay. The court allowed the evidence admitted, and defendants excepted.

P. A. Martin and John Speer also took a heavy beating. Certified copies of Martin's conviction in North Carolina and two previous larceny convictions of Speer in Tarrant County, Texas, in 1883, on which he had received two terms of imprisonment of two years each, were produced by the defense. The government, in turn, read into evidence a full proclamation of pardon for Speer's offenses, and that Martin had served his sentence in the Iredell County jail. Defendants objected because "under the laws of Texas witnesses were incompetent to testify by virtue of an express statute," and because "the offenses for which they were convicted being infamous crimes, they are incompetent to testify in the United States court held within the State of Texas." Judge McCormick overruled these objections and admitted their testimony as "material facts." Defendants "excepted to the admission, and to the instruction of the court thereon."[10]

The court also admitted, against like objections and exceptions, the statements of Collier, Hollis and others made while in pursuit of the Marlows and during the siege at the Denson farm that Logan was not a guard and must have been the person who informed the mob of the intended removal of the prisoners to Weatherford; that Logan was one of the conspirators and a leader in the attack at Dry Creek, and had been wounded there. Defendants maintained that such declarations were not made in Logan's presence, and were made "some on the same night and others some days after the fight."[11]

Defendants' attorneys clashed strongly with McCormick in requesting the judge to instruct the jury that "the matters alleged in the indictments and the proof made under them constituted no offense under the laws of the United States, and, therefore, they should return a verdict of not guilty." Judge McCormick refused, and before delivering his charge to the jury, "felt constrained" to note some of the features of the "very extraordinary speech" made by Colonel Kearby in summing up the evidence:

> In the conclusion of his speech, the counsel charged you to lay your heads on the breasts of the wives and friends of the defendants and hear their life blood drop, drop, drop in their hearts agonized unutterably by suspense during your deliberations — and merit their

prayers for God's blessing on you by acquitting these defendants. This was dramatic and pathetic, but it is not an argument on the law or the facts of this case, such as should be addressed to intelligent and virtuous men engaged in the discharge of the highest and most solemn duty. . . .

Mr. Kearby also challenged your experience to answer if you had ever known a case where such a mass of hearsay evidence was given to a jury and charged that you were under no obligation to consider this testimony — that this was a matter over which you had exclusive control, and over which the court — meaning the Judge — had none. Now in some States — in Illinois, for instance — the jury in a criminal case are the judges of the law and of the facts, but no man knows better than Mr. Kearby that in Texas, and in this Court, the jury are in no instance judges of the law but must receive the law from the Court, and that whether there is evidence, or what is evidence? is always a question of law and to be determined by the Judge. Therefore all that the Judge permitted to be given you is to be considered by you and your sole province is to determine what it proves. . . .

The whole tone and fiber of this counsel's cross-examination of many of the Government's witnesses and the web and woof of his speech to the jury was pregnant with the charge that there was something behind this prosecution, with the innuendo that the chief officers of this Court had combined to suborn witnesses to compound felonies to sweep the country for convicted criminals and persons accused of crime to swear away the lives or liberties of these defendants. There is not a word or syllable or letter or character capable of making the least impression on any intelligent and impartial mind tending in the slightest degree to support these insinuations and innuendos.

Mr. Kearby also expressed his high approval of the

mob feeling that some witnesses thought existed here and pronounced a labored encomium on all who may have participated in that feeling. We do not live in newly discovered gold fields to which men have flocked and where they have commenced a life of labor without organized government or law for their security, neither are we any longer rangers on a boundless range remote from the machinery of civil government, but in a fully organized community, and at the very spot where Justice has opened her temples to give relief and protection to all who love her. Her courts are amply and fully equipped with officers. Mr. Kearby, as an attorney, bears her commission as one of her officers. You are duly selected, impaneled and sworn helpers at her altars, and when this stab is made at her vitals, Justice may well take up Immanuel's burden and cry: "I am wounded in the house of my friends. My own familiar friend in whom I trusted has lifted up his hand against me."[12]

Judge McCormick then instructed the jury:

When a citizen of the United States is committed to the custody of a United States marshal, or to a state jail, by process issuing from one of the courts in the United States, to be held, in default of bail, to await his trial on a criminal charge within the exclusive jurisdiction of the national courts, such citizen has a right, under the Constitution and laws of the United States, to a speedy and public trial by an impartial jury, and, until tried or discharged by due process of law, has the right, under said Constitution and laws, to be treated with humanity, and to be protected against all unlawful violence, while he is deprived of the ordinary means of defending and protecting himself.

McCormick further defined the crimes charged — conspiracy and murder in the prosecution of the conspiracy — and submitted the question whether the defendants were guilty of the conspiracy only, or guilty of murder also.[13]

A verdict was rendered at 6 o'clock Friday evening, April 17:

> We, the jury in Consolidated Case No. 34, United States vs. Eugene Logan and others, find the defendants Eugene Logan, Sam Waggoner and Marion Wallace guilty of the conspiracy as charged in the indictment, and we further find said defendants not guilty of murder as charged in the indictment.
>
> We, the jury further find the defendants Dick Cook, John Levell, Will Hollis, Verna Wilkerson not guilty.
>
> G. R. Patton
Foreman of Jury.[14]

Said the *Graham Leader*:

> The verdict gave misery and suffering to some and joy and peace to others. . . . Cook and Wilkerson immediately left and were soon in the bosom of their happy families. Hollis, who is a single man, was soon on the streets shaking hands with his friends. Levell, who has been quite sick during the trial, was driven to the home of Mrs. Wallace, where with tender and watchful care . . . we have every reason to hope for his speedy recovery from the effects of his long confinement.[15]

The defense moved for a rehearing of the case, listing eleven special exceptions, which the court denied individually.[16] Logan, Waggoner and Wallace were brought into court Saturday morning, April 18. In passing sentence Judge McCormick said:

> From personal observation . . . as well as from the development of this trial, my mind is fully imbued with the knowledge of the existence, spirit, extent and power

of a local combination here to prevent the judicial dis-
covery and punishment of the conspirators who slew the
Marlows at Dry Creek — a combination which has largely perverted or paralyzed not only the power of this
county, but to some extent of the adjoining counties,
and so leveled its threatening and aggressive force against
the regular officers of this court as to justify and require
the employment of special assistance to meet it and to
call for the utmost vigilance and faithfulness on the part
of the all who are set for the vindication and enforcement of the laws.

In view of this state of the case, wholly unexampled in
. . . nearly twenty years that I have held judicial office . . .
it becomes my solemn duty to pronounce the sentence
of the court that each of you be fined $5,000, and that
each of you be imprisoned for the term of ten years, and
that each of you shall hereafter by ineligible to any office
or place of honor, profit or trust created by the
Constitution and laws of the United States.[17]

To a *Dallas News* correspondent, McCormick commented:
"This is the first time in the annals of history where unarmed
prisoners, shackled together, ever repelled a mob. Such cool
courage that preferred to fight against such great odds and
die, if at all, in glorious battle rather than die ignominiously
. . . deserves to be commemorated in song and story."

Marshal Knight took the prisoners to Fort Worth, where he
delivered them into the care and custody of the jailer of
Tarrant County, first demanding the sum of $5,000 from
each, payment of which was refused, and no property
found.[18]

XIV

Governor Routt Takes A Hand

George and Charles Marlow
returned to Colorado, feeling unavenged but hopeful that this
lesson of retribution would not be lost on the acquitted and
others who more or less had been connected with the false
accusations, brutal treatment and wounds inflicted upon
them. However, the curtain was not ready to fall upon the
drama of the mob's misdeeds.

Logan, Waggoner and Wallace, by their attorneys, filed a
bill of exceptions listing thirty-three actions of the court in
refusing a request or overruling an objection during the trial,
and sued out a writ of error "to the end that a transcript of
the proceedings had in this case may be certified to the
Supreme Court of the United States . . . to review and revise
the errors complained of herein."[1] A petition for bail was
denied by Judge McCormick and defendants petitioned the

135

Honorable Don A. Pardee, judge of the 5th Circuit Court, Northern District of Texas, for a writ of habeas corpus, alleging illegal restraint by U. S. Marshal Knight, "because the indictments under which they were convicted charge defendants with no offense against the laws of the United States, and because the averments in said indictments show the offenses therein described are within the exclusive jurisdiction of the State of Texas." Judge Pardee denied the writ, stating that "petitioners are entitled to carry their case to the Supreme Court of the United States for review by writ of error and are still in time to obtain a supersedeas and release on bail under the rules of that Court."[2]

On June 27, the transcript of the trial and proceedings of the Graham court was filed in the office of Supreme Court Clerk James H. McKenney, with writ of error, allowed by Judge McCormick, and a citation of error, signed by Judge McCormick, attached. On July 29, Associate Justice L. Q. C. Lamar ordered Logan, Waggoner and Wallace admitted to bail, "upon their giving bond for their appearance in the Supreme Court . . . at the first day of the next [October 1891] term, in the sum of ten thousand dollars ($10,000) each, the security to be approved by the clerk of the United States Circuit Court for the Northern District of Texas, or the District Judge."[3]

On August 14, seven wealthy stockmen of Young County appeared before U. S. Commissioner Girand, pledging themselves jointly and severally for the $10,000 bail for Sam Waggoner. The bond was approved and filed by Clerk Finks and Waggoner was released from the Tarrant County jail.[4]

Waggoner and his friends lost no time getting the ear of the Texas attorney general, who obtained a state requisition for the arrest of George and Charles Marlow on the Young County indictment charging complicity in the killing of Sheriff Wallace by Boone Marlow in December 1888. The requisition was placed in the hands of William Jesse "Bill" McDonald and A. J. Britton, two of the state's most fearless Rangers.

In his nearly fifteen years as a deputy sheriff in Wood and Hardeman counties, deputy U. S. marshal of the Northern District of Texas, and now captain of Company B, Frontier Battalion of the Rangers, McDonald had become a legend. His bold tactics had driven the Brookins gang from Hardeman County, and his raids on cattle thieves and train robbers in the Panhandle at large had done much to establish a condition of proper behavior in the area. He was ranked as one of the state's best all-around marksmen, and for the other fellow to begin shooting was considered equivalent to suicide.

Both Rangers knew the Marlows and were aware of their courage and ability with firearms in a desperate fight. Nonetheless, they were representatives of the State of Texas and had a duty to perform.

A few days after receiving the requisition, McDonald and Britton — bronzed, handsome men, armed with the latest Colt revolvers swung from heavily-loaded cartridge belts — stepped off the Denver & Rio Grande train onto the depot platform at Ridgway, Colorado. They informed Sheriff J. H. Bradley of Ouray County of the purpose of their mission. Under the law, it was necessary that the local sheriff make the arrest and turn the prisoners over to the Rangers for conveyance and delivery to the Young County, Texas, authorities.

The Marlows were doing their best to pick up the pieces of their shattered lives and had gained wide respect in the area. Sheriff Bradley was one of their best friends.

Bradley crossed the foothills to the Marlow ranch. A Winchester rifle covered his towering figure long before he came within hailing distance, for the brothers were ever on the alert. When the sheriff was recognized, a hearty welcome was tendered him. He told George and Charles why he was there and advised them to accompany him to Ridgway and have a talk with the Rangers.

"We've had a bellyful of Texas justice," George said. "We will go to Ridgway but do not intend to be taken back to Young County under any circumstance. If matters cannot be

137

arranged to prevent it, will you stand aside and let the Rangers try to arrest us themselves?"

"Do you know Captain McDonald and Britton?" the sheriff asked.

"Yes," George replied. "They are good men and would be hard to down if it came to battle. They have no doubt made up their minds to take us. But we would no sooner reach Texas than we would be set upon by the same mob that shot our brothers all to pieces, and never live to stand trial. If we have to be killed, let it be here. At least, we will receive a decent burial."

"I don't blame you," Bradley said. "By no act of mine shall you boys ever go back there to be murdered."[5]

McDonald and Britton, in the meantime, had gone by train twelve miles to Ouray, leaving word that they would return on the next train with proper papers for releasing the Marlows into their custody.

Rumor spread about Ridgway that the Rangers intended to take the Marlows with or without waiver of extradition, and little groups of armed men began to assemble along the streets in whispered consultation. The Marlows had proved themselves to be good citizens, and it was given out that if Texas wanted to take them from Colorado "she had better send up 2,000 men instead of two Rangers." When the train came snorting down the mountain grade, a large crowd was waiting at the depot. "The baggageman forgot to throw in the trunks, the station agent never thought of carrying out telegraph orders to the conductor or engineer, and Jack Brown, the best known and best liked conductor in the San Juan country, forgot for the first time in twenty years to call out his stentorian, 'All aboard!'" Every eye was on the Rangers as they stepped upon the platform, and on George and Charles Marlow standing beside Sheriff Bradley, their backs to the station wall and gun hands ready for action.[6]

McDonald and Britton strode briskly to the Marlows, nodding and extending their left hands. George and Charles extended their left hands. It was a left-handed shake all around.

"You boys know why we are here," McDonald said. "We do not want any trouble or hard feelings at all, and trust you will go with us peaceably."

"That will be up to the governor at Denver," replied Charles. "It will take a little time, but after that we will discuss going with you as prisoners."

Sheriff Bradley accompanied the party to Denver, riding in the rear of the coach with George and Charles, who kept the Rangers in view at all times. At Denver, the Rangers repaired to a hotel, the Marlows sleeping in the stations agent's office. Next morning, Governor John L. Routt was presented the facts. He was already familiar with the Marlows' troubles. It was the opinion of Colorado's state attorney that the brothers, being deputized federal officers and under jurisdiction of the United States courts as government witnesses, were not amenable to the local courts of Texas, or any other state. He telegraphed the Texas attorney general, who acknowledged that the brothers were still under federal protection. Governor Routt refused to recognize the requisition.

McDonald and Britton "took the matter philosophically." They shook hands with the Colorado officials, wished George and Charles Marlow "good luck and prosperity," and departed on the east-bound train without their quarry.[7]

The Graham Court Faulted

At the October 1891 term of the Supreme Court in Washington, No. 34, Consolidated, was argued as *Eugene Logan et al., Plaintiffs in Error vs. United States.*[1] The court ruled specifically on eight of the thirty-three exceptions taken by plaintiffs' attorneys to the rulings and instructions of Judge A. P. McCormick:

> The right of a citizen in custody of a United States marshal under a lawful commitment for an offense against the United States, to be protected against lawless violence, was a right secured within the meaning of Revised Statute 5508. It was "a crime to conspire to injure, etc. any citizen in the free exercise or enjoyment of such right."

When there are "several charges against any person for the same act or transaction, or for two or more acts or trans-actions of the same class of crime or offense," they may be "properly joined . . . in one indictment in separate counts, and if two or more indictments are found in such cases, the court "may order them to be consolidated." The objection to consolidation of the indictments on which plaintiffs in error were tried and convicted "cannot prevail."

Under Act of February 24, 1879, creating the northern judicial district of Texas, and amendment of Section 5 by Act of June 14, 1880, providing that all prosecutions shall be tried in that division, to which process for the county in which the offenses are committed is required to be returned, and that all writs and recognizances shall be turned to the division to which the prosecutions are to be tried, "does not affect the authority of the grand jury for the district sitting at any place at which the court is appointed to be held to present indictments for offenses committed anywhere within the district." Objection to the four indictments that they should have been found by the grand jury at Graham, and not at Dallas, "is based on a misapprehension of the acts of congress upon this subject."

A plea of former jeopardy showing that the jury on a former trial was discharged, without defendants' consent and by the court on its own motion, after the jury had announced that they were unable to agree, "is bad on its face." The discharge of the jury was "a question to be decided by the presiding judge in the sound exercise of his discretion."

On the trial of defendant for a crime punishable by death, where the jury is to find the punishment, jurors who state on their *voir dire* that they have conscientious scruples in regard to infliction of the death penalty for crime "may be challenged for cause by the government." A juror who has conscientious scruples on any subject, which prevents him from standing indifferent between the government and the accused, "is not an impartial juror."

The competency of witnesses in criminal trials in the federal courts in Texas "is not governed by the statutes of the state passed since its admission into the Union, but by common law, which was the law of Texas at the time of its admission." The provision of the Revised Statutes of the United States that the laws of the state in which the court is held shall be the rules of decision as to the competency of witnesses who had been previously convicted and sentenced for felony "is not applicable to criminal trials, such trials not being embraced within the words 'at common law.'" At common law, and on general principles of jurisprudence, when not controlled by express statute, "such conviction and sentence can have no effect by way of penalty or of personal disability or qualification beyond the limits of the state in which the judgment is rendered." The conviction of P. A.Martin in North Carolina "does not make the convict incompetent to testify in Texas." The competency of Speer to testify "is equally clear . . . he was convicted and sentenced in Texas, and the full pardon of the governor of the state, although granted after he had served out his term of imprisonment, thenceforth took away all disqualifications as a witness, and restored his competency to testify to any facts within his knowledge before the disqualification had been removed by pardon."

Eugene Logan, Sam Waggoner and Marion Wallace would have gone to prison had not the Supreme Court faulted Judge McCormick on the points as follows:

Section 1033 of the Revised Statutes provided: "When any person is indicted of treason, a copy of the indictment, and a list of the jury, and of the witnesses to be produced on the trial for proving the indictment, stating the place of abode of each juror and witness, shall be delivered to him at least three entire days before he is tried for the same. When any person is indicted of any other capital offense, such copy of the indictment and list of jurors and witnesses shall be delivered to him at least two entire days before the trial." This provision "is not directory only, but *mandatory* to the government."

In all cases of conspiracy, "the act of one conspirator in the prosecution of the enterprise is considered the act of all, and is evidence against all. . . . But only those acts and declarations are admissible under this rule which are done and made while the conspiracy is pending, and in furtherance of its object. After the conspiracy has come to an end, whether by success or by failure, the admissions of one conspirator by way of narrative of past facts, are not admissible in evidence against the others. . . . Even if, as suggested by the counsel of the United States, the conspiracy included an attempt to manufacture evidence to shield Logan . . . subsequent declarations that Logan acted with the mob at the fight at Dry Creek after the fight was over, were incompetent in any view of the case. . . . The court went too far in admitting testimony on the general question of conspiracy. . . . The admission of incompetent evidence of such acts of Logan prejudiced all the defendants."

Accordingly, on April 4, 1892, the Supreme Court reversed and remanded the cause to the Graham court, with directions to set aside the verdict and order a new trial.[2]

XVI

Colorado Sunset

No. 34, Consolidated, *United States vs. Eugene Logan et al.* was never retried, but it left Young County torn and divided — in politics, business and even in churches. Many citizens demanded that those who had put themselves above the law be punished. Others were afraid to express themselves, pro or con, and thought it best to forget the entire matter and begin anew.

While attending court at Graham in March 1891, George and Charles Marlow had discussed with a Dallas attorney the possibility of damage suits against the mob participants. The attorney advised that, since Ed Johnson had been implicated and was under direct commission of ex-U.S. Marshal Cabell, they should include Cabell and the sureties on his official bond. The suits brought were: Martha Marlow, on account of the murder of her son Epp, $10,000; Zenia Marlow, widow of Alf, on account of his murder, $10,000; George and Charles, on account of the wounds they had suffered, $10,000 each.[1]

These cases dragged on for months. Johnson appeared as a witness several times at Dallas. George and Charles were hesitant to "blame him" — he had "done all he could for them at Dry Creek," though his guards had "failed in their duty." This, together with the brothers' refusal to answer the state charge of complicity in the killing of Sheriff Wallace, resulted in the suits being dropped, with a compromise. George was awarded damages of $1,000, and Charles, $1,950. Martha and Zenia received nothing.[2]

In 1893, after Grover Cleveland was inaugurated for his second term as president of the United States and the Northern District of Texas was taken over by a Democratic administration, the mob cases were ended by dismissal or *nolle prosequi*. Most of the principals faded from the picture. Sam Waggoner had contracted tuberculosis while in jail at Dallas and died at Graham. Verna Wilkerson sold his ranch and moved to Wilbarger County, where he was killed in a dispute over a cattle sale shortly before the turn of the century. Robert Holman moved to Austin, where he practiced law until his death at age forty. Jack Wilkins continued to ranch in Young County until his death at age sixty-seven. John Levell married the widow of Bee Williams, left Graham and is thought to have died years later in Pecos County. Eugene Logan became an inspector for the Cattlemen's Association of West Texas and finally proprietor of a rooming house at Dalhart. Ed Johnson never regained full use of his left hand. His wife taught music at home to make ends meet. He served as office deputy under O. H. Brown, sheriff of Young County, from 1911 to 1914, then moved to Los Angeles, where he worked in the civil department of the sheriff's office for fifteen years; he died in the early 1930s.

Talk of moving the federal court from Graham, begun in November 1889, was revived under the Cleveland administration. Articles published in the Texas press, the *New York Times* and the romantically imaginative *National Police Gazette* depicted Young County as wild and uncivilized.[3] James Stephen Hogg, who succeeded Sul Ross as governor in 1891, did nothing to quiet the controversy.

Governor Hogg had fought government corruption throughout his career as a newspaperman, lawyer, and county and district attorney, and many times had called for a more careful administration of federal laws in Texas. In his first message to the state legislature, he spelled out the conditions that he believed existed:

> For many years our people have been terrorized by the judicial arm of the government, not for offenses they have committed, but because they dread the menace of arbitrary power that so often threatens their liberties. . . . Deputy marshals, special detectives and others asserting authority have infested the populous as well as the remote regions of this state, unnecessarily disturbing the tranquility of the people, and by their misconduct and association with spies and informers have caused many to believe our federal government an institution of oppression instead of one for the performance of the functions under the constitution. . . . Numerous citizens have been arrested and carried many miles from their homes on frivolous charges of which they were not guilty.[4]

The governor further recommended "an appropriation to be placed in the hands of the executive department to protect Texas and her people from unjust prosecutions and encroachment of the federal courts." His strong language "raised eyebrows in Washington and a howl of indignation from petty federal officers in the state."[5]

Nonetheless, Young County had experienced great growth and achieved prestige during the years the federal court was at Graham. Judge McCormick's wisdom, integrity and ideals

were an inspiration to the citizens of the little city; his deci-
sions and opinions would be referred to for years to come.[6] In
1892 he was promoted to circuit judge at Dallas and succeeded at Graham by John B. Rector, former judge of the Thirty-
first Judicial District.

Republican leaders of Young County prepared maps and
tabulated and compared the population of counties throughout the district, but they had lost much influence in
Washington and were unable to combat the pressure from the
booming railroad centers of Abilene and Fort Worth. With
the increase of settlement, Congress saw a need for an additional court and, early in 1896, passed a bill creating one at
Fort Worth and moving the Graham court to Abilene.[7]

George and Charles Marlow never saw Texas again. Tax
assessment rolls of Ouray County, Colorado, for the late
1890s show they and their families variously operated irrigat-
ed and dry farmlands three miles southwest and five miles
west-southwest of Ridgway, on Billy Creek southeast of
Colona, and owned residential lots in Ridgway. Listed among
their assets were a number of horses, cows, sheep, swine, wagons and road vehicles.

George and Charles also performed deputy work for Ouray
County's new sheriff, Maurice Corbett. On one occasion,
George was notified to intercept two men accused of a dry-
goods theft in Telluride. George met the pair four miles outside of Montrose, recovered the contraband, and jailed them
until train time. He then took them to Ridgway, where he
expected to meet the Telluride officer. Instead, he found a
telegram declaring them to be desperate men and instructing
him to chain them to a seat in the passenger car and bring
them to Telluride on the evening train.

George had his own ideas about the way the prisoners
should be treated, partly from his sense of justice and partly
from the Texas experience yet vivid in his memory. Instead of

The George and Charles Marlow families in Colorado, 1897. Left to right: Myrtle, Elisha, Dottie, Josephine, Lillian, George Marlow, Martha Jane Marlow (seated), Charles Marlow holding Georgia, Emma, Alpha, Charles, Jr., Mattie, and Margarita.

complying with the telegram, he took the men home where his wife prepared supper for all.

After supper, Charles brought in a prisoner named Ed Best and asked George to hold him until Sheriff Corbett could come down and take him to Ouray the next morning. Best boasted that his friends would rescue him before daybreak. George thought otherwise and handcuffed the three prisoners together. They went to bed on the floor and slept — some. After breakfast, Corbett arrived for Best. George took his prisoners by train to Dallas Divide, where he met the Telluride sheriff, who was considerably disturbed that George had taken such chances.

A year later, one of the men, having served his sentence, met George in Ridgway. He was broke, hungry and barefooted. George bought him a pair of shoes and worked him for two weeks in the hayfield. Upon leaving, the man resolved to change his course in life on the basis of the treatment George had given him as a prisoner and a hired man.[8]

The Marlows especially remembered the time in December 1891 when they were summoned by Sheriff Doc Shores to assist in a miners strike at Crested Butte, a coal camp of 1500 population in Gunnison County. Five hundred workers, predominantly Austrian and Italian immigrants, lived there in cramped boardinghouses and shacks. Their wages had been drastically cut by the Colorado Coal & Iron Company due to a reduction in the selling price of coke to meet increased competition from Utah mines and the lower price on locomotive coal offered by the Denver & Rio Grande Railroad. Much violence already had erupted.

George and Charles were not advised of the details. They boarded the train to Gunnison City because Doc Shores was a friend and needed help.

They reached Gunnison at dusk, clad in heavy suits, big hats and knee-high boots, wearing .45 Colt single-action six-shooters in Mexican loop holsters that passed freely over cartridge-laden belts, and carrying sawed-off Winchesters. Hungry, and desirous of observing the city's proprieties rela-

tive to carrying firearms, they asked the station agent to check
their weapons until they ate supper.

As the agent took their guns, he inquired: "What are you
boys doing?"

"Just drifting," George said.

"You had better keep on drifting," the agent advised, "or
Sheriff Shores will get you and lock you up."

"Why, he's the very man we want to see," Charles said.

While they were at supper, the agent telegraphed Shores
that two bank robbers or desperadoes were in town looking
for him. Shores wired back to send these bank robbers or desperadoes by special train to Crested Butte at once.

When George and Charles claimed their weapons, the
agent asked if they were those two "hell-roarin'" Marlows he
had been reading about, to which Charles modestly replied:
"Our names are Marlow."9

The special train was soon ready, and they were off to
Crested Butte as fast as its crew, with several delays because of
snow, could take them.

They found Shores in the superintendent's building, with
sixty some men, "scabs" the miners called them, who were
willing to go to work when the sheriff and coal company officials could assure them safety. They were blocked by a party of
armed toughs, who did not work in the mine but claimed to
be there to help the downtrodden workers obtain their rights.
The fans in the mine had been shut down, the mine was fill-
ing up with dangerous coal gas, and an explosion was immi-
nent unless the fans could be started again.

It was a ticklish situation, but Shores thought he knew a solution. He liked these hard-working, hard-drinking miners and
prized their friendship. They had every right to strike, he told
them, but he was disappointed over outside toughs handling
their affairs. Drinking was the favorite and about the only
amusement in Crested Butte. Shores invited the so-called "pro-
tectors" to one of the bars to discuss matters like civilized men.

Once they were inside, Shores closed the door. He and

Left to right: George Marlow, "Doc" Shores, and Charles Marlow during the Crested Butte miners' strike, December 1891.

George Marlow covered the toughs from behind with six-shooters and Winchesters. Charles leaped onto the bar before them, his .45 Colt leveled, and said: "We are for peace, but if any man pulls a gun, he will regret it!" The vantage point of Shores and the Marlows soon won a favorable opinion. Seven ringleaders were led to an improvised bastille to await transportation to the Gunnison jail. Within a few days, the fans in the mine were restarted and the miners were back on their jobs. George and Charles returned to Ridgway, and a week later, they received a carload of winter coal for their services in the Crested Butte strike.[10]

Charles and Emma Marlow raised five daughters and a son. George and Lillian raised one son and three daughters. In 1899, George was paid a tribute that recognized not only his sterling qualities but also his affectionate interest in the children of his community — he was elected president of School District No. 3 in Ouray County. On September 27, 1904, the first of the Marlow children married — George's daughter Myrtle took for her husband L. C. Mills of Ouray. Said the *Montrose Enterprise* of September 30: "Rev. Marsh performed the ceremony in the home of the bride's parents. Scores of friends were present and numerous gifts were received by the happy couple."

Martha Marlow was failing, despite the watchful care of George and Charles and their families. She had weathered the storms of border life — lost more and won more perhaps than any woman of her time. Eyes that had ever been alert lost their sparkle. For weeks she remarked on the weariness she felt but always concluded by speaking of the comfort she had in the now-settled affairs of her sons. She died October 7, 1907, and was laid to rest on a knoll on the Billy Creek farm.

Charles remained on his place near Ridgway. George sold his Billy Creek property and moved to Montrose. He was now in his fifties, and a grandfather — "Gramps" his youngest daughter called him. He had a habit of renaming everyone with whom he became acquainted, with a special deference for the ladies. The older ones he categorized as "Auntie," the younger ones, "Sister." Dusk was his bedtime, his costume a sleeping shirt, socks and longjohns.

Each of his daughters learned to expect, when entertaining a boyfriend in the parlor at a late hour, to be confronted by Gramps who would rouse from his slumber, stand just out of the light, rubbing his eyes, sleeping shirt dangling around the baggy knees of his underwear and socks askew, and softly ask, "Ain't it time you was in bed, Sister?" It was his way of suggesting the caller should go home. But next day he would indelicately inquire, "Sister, did he kiss you good night?"[11]

And this from the *Montrose Daily Press* after President Woodrow Wilson delivered his war message to Congress April 2, 1917, and Congress passed the war declaration against Germany: "George Marlow, famous old timer and pioneer, has applied at the local board for a chance to go to France to enter any military service that the government can give him. His age is the only bar. . . . He has a long white beard, which makes him look older than he is. He says he has never been sick and can march or fight or drive trucks or anything else all day without fatigue."

In 1916, Charles bought "sort of a half-way house" between his old ranch and Montrose, the *Montrose Press* of June 28 reported. "Mr. Marlow says he knows nothing about placer mining . . . but the other day he went out and tried his hand in the bed of the river on his place where the sand has been deposited for a long time. He panned a few shovelfuls and got 17 colors of flake gold. This so encouraged him that he will try his luck again in a more systematic way. There is a lot of placer gold in the river and on the hillside near the mouth of Cow Creek, and some placer mining was done there 30 years ago. A man can make wages panning the dirt almost anywhere along there. Some day the lead from which this gold comes will be uncovered and it will prove a bonanza."

Charles never uncovered the hoped-for "bonanza." He and Emma retired to Glendale, California, in 1922. All their children were married, two living in Montrose, the rest in

154

Glendale, Oakland and Los Angeles. Charles reportedly was "comfortably fixed. . . . He and his wife who has shared all the sorrows of earlier days are traveling the Western Slope . . . 'pals' in the truest sense of the word."[12] They were residing in Los Angeles when Charles suffered a bout with influenza and died at age eighty, on January 19, 1941.

George and Lillian retired in 1929. They had "little of this world's goods, but enough and some to spare to the down-and-outs that seem to deserve"; their children, too, were married and "as much settled in life as the old folks ever were, with a heritage of honesty and hospitality that will never cease while memory lasts."[13] They celebrated their golden wedding anniversary in the spacious rooms of the Elks' home at Montrose on June 17, 1933.

Said the *Montrose Daily Press*:

> The hall was decorated in a color motif of gold and white, which predominated the tables as well. Tables were arranged in the shape of a horseshoe, Mr. and Mrs. Marlow occupying the center. At this point a gold and white wedding cake was placed. In the center of the cake was a cupid, befitting a love that had endured half a century of sorrow and gladness. On either side of the cake were candlelabras. Over the heads of this beloved couple hung an illuminated golden wedding bell.
>
> At 7 o'clock, surrounded by all their children, grandchildren and great grandchildren, a banquet was served, with outside relatives and guests present. Following the banquet and toast, the hall was cleared and dancing was enjoyed to the music of the Colona orchestra until midnight. Many friends from distant cities attended the affair.

Lillian Marlow died October 19, 1936, at age seventy, while visiting a daughter and son-in-law in Denver. Following her death, George made his home in Denver, spending a great

Marlow family descendants, 1915. The photo was taken at Charles Marlow's home in Colorado.

deal of time visiting his other children and old friends around Montrose, He died in St. Luke's Hospital at Montrose of "cardiac recompensation" July 3, 1945, within a month of his ninetieth birthday, and was laid to rest beside his wife in Denver's Crown Hill cemetery.

In his last days, George spoke often of the killings at Dry Creek, but would come out of these moments of reverie to sigh: "I love everybody — I ain't got a enemy in the world." Sometimes, however, memories flamed too high; he would massage the old wound in his right hand and growl angrily: "I'd go a hundred miles to shoot a mob!"[14]

Notes

Chapter I

1. For the wanderings and adventures of the Marlow family, 1804-1886, see *Life of the Marlows, A True Story of Frontier Life in the Early Days* (hereafter cited as *Life of the Marlows*), as Related by Themselves. (Ouray, Colorado: Ouray Herald Print, W. S. Olexa, Publisher, 1928), pp. 7-17, 25-26, 85-88; also testimony of Charles and George Marlow, Case No. 34, Consolidated, *United States vs. Eugene Logan, Verna Wilkerson, and Clint Rutherford*, U.S. District Court, Graham, Texas, October term 1890 (all federal records and trial transcripts can be found at the Fort Worth, Texas, Federal Records Center).

Brief summaries of the early life of the Marlows appear in Charles A. Siringo, *Riata and Spurs: The Story of a Lifetime Spent in the Saddle as Cowboy and Ranger* (New York and Boston: Houghton Mifflin, 1927), pp. 206-07; William MacLeod Raine, *Famous Sheriffs and Western Outlaws* (New York: Doubleday, Doran, 1929), pp. 26-27; "The Historical Saga of the Marlow Brothers," *Montrose* (Colorado) *Daily Press*, March 10, 1988.

Several passages in the Marlow narrative required historical verification, which was obtained from the following sources:

Mary Neely Capps, "The Navajo Peaks," *Oklahoma Today*, vol. 27, no. 2, Spring 1977; Edward Everett Dale, "Old Navajoe," *Chronicles of Oklahoma*, vol. 24, no. 2, Summer 1946, pp. 128-45; Llerena Friend, "Wichita Falls, Texas," *The Handbook of Texas* (Austin: Texas State Historical Association, 1952), vol. 2, pp. 903-04; H. H. Halsell, *Cowboys and Cattleland* (Nashville, Tennessee:

The Parthenon Press, 1937 [reprinted by Texas Christian University Press, 1983]), pp. 128-32; "Historical Notes," *Chronicles of Oklahoma*, vol. 20, no. 2, June 1942, pp. 190-91; "Historical Notes and Comments," *Chronicles of Oklahoma*, vol. 20, no. 3, September 1942, pp. 303-05; "Marlow, a Rapidly Growing City with a Most Brilliant Future," *Daily Oklahoman*, June 3, 1906; *Oklahoma, A Guide to the Sooner State*. American Guide Series. (Norman: University of Oklahoma Press, 1941), 374; Eleanor Pace, "Wilbarger County," *The Handbook of Texas*, vol. 2, pp. 908-09; Hobart D. Ragland, *This History of Rush Springs* (Rush Springs, Oklahoma: Gazette Publishing Company, 1952), pp. 11-31; Carl Coke Rister, *No Man's Land* (Norman: University of Oklahoma Press, 1948), pp. 46-53, 67-71; Wilson Rockwell (editor), *Memoirs of A Lawman* (Denver: Sage Books, 1952), pp. 24-134 *passim*, 139, 186; Wilbur Fiske Stone (editor), *History of Colorado* (Chicago: S. J. Clarke Publishing Company, 1918), vol. 1, pp. 18, 156, 287-88, 478-81, 488-93, 838-40; Ralph C. Taylor, *Colorado South of the Border* (Denver: Sage Books, 1963), pp. 253-58, 323-29.

2. Halsell, *Cowboys and Cattleland*, pp. 128-32.

3. *Life of the Marlows*, pp. 18-20.

4. *Ibid.*, pp. 87-88.

5. *Ibid.*, p. 21.

6. *Ibid.*, pp. 21-22.

7. *Ibid.*, p. 89.

Chapter II

1. Sources for the founding, organization and growth of Young County, Fort Belknap, Belknap town and county seat of Graham:

Sam Acheson, "Great Hanging at Gainesville," *The Handbook of Texas-A Supplement*, vol. 3, p. 321; Thomas Barrett, *The Great Hanging at Gainesville, Texas* (Austin: Reprint by Texas State Historical Asociation, 1961), pp. 3-34; "Belknap, Texas," *The Handbook of Texas*, vol. 1, p. 140; "County Named for Colonel Wm Young," *Graham News*, August 24, 1967; Carrie J. Crouch, *A History of Young County, Texas* (Austin: Texas States Historical Association, 1956), pp. 108-15, 125-28, 137; "Fort Belknap," *The Handbook of Texas*, vol. 1, p. 620; "Graham, Texas," *The Handbook of Texas*, vol. 1, pp. 714-15; L. W. Kemp, "William Cocke Young,"

The Handbook of Texas, vol. 2, pp. 947-48; "Peace Party Conspiracy," *The Handbook of Texas*, vol. 2, p. 348; R. N. Richardson, "Robert Simpson Neighbors," *The Handbook of Texas*, vol. 2, pp. 267-68; "Young County," *The Handbook of Texas*, vol. 2, pp. 948-49.

Sources for creation of the Northern District of Texas and Graham division, attachment of western portion of Indian Territory, and sketches of federal court and Young County officials:

"Andrew Phelps McCormick," *The Handbook of Texas*, vol. 2, p. 104; Crouch, *A History of Young County, Texas*, pp. 121, 113-14; William C. Davis (editor), *The Confederate General* (n.p.: A Publication of the National Historical Society, 1991), vol. 1, pp. 155-57; *Graham Leader*, March 14, 1889; "Outstanding Jurist Held First Federal Court," *Graham News*, May 5, 1974; Testimony of P. A. Martin, Case No. 34, Consolidated, *United States vs. Eugene Logan, Verna Wilkerson and Clint Rutherford*, U.S. District Court, Graham, Texas, October term 1890; John William Rogers, *The Lusty Texans of Dallas* (New York: E. P. Dutton, 1951), pp. 185-87; William S. Speer (editor), *The Encyclopedia of the New West* (Marshall, Texas: United States Biographical Publishing Company, 1881), pp. 375-76; "William Lewis Cabell," *The Handbook of Texas*, vol. 1, p. 261.

2. *Graham Leader*, December 27, 1888.

Chapter III

1. Message of Governor James Stephen Hogg to the Texas state legislature in January 1891 (*Graham Leader*, February 4, 1891).

2. Raine, *Famous Sheriffs and Western Outlaws*, p. 27; William MacLeod Raine and Will C. Barnes, *Cattle* (New York: Doubleday, Doran, 1930), p. 188; C. L. Sonnichsen, *I'll Die Before I'll Run: The Story of the Great Feuds of Texas* (New York: Harper and Brothers, 1951), p. 156.

3. Robert L. Brown, *An Empire of Silver* (Caldwell, Idaho: Caxton Printers, 1965), p. 121.

4. *Life of the Marlows*, pp. 27-28.

5. Case No. 238, *United States vs. Alf Marlow et al.*, U.S. Commissioners Court, Graham, Texas, filed August 18, 1888.

6. *Life of the Marlows*, p. 30. Martha Marlow provides details of the arrest of Boone, Epp and young Metz, pp. 28-30.

7. Testimony of Charles Marlow in No. 34, Consolidated, *United States vs. Eugene Logan, Verna Wilkerson and Clint Rutherford*, U.S. District Court, Graham, Texas, October term 1890; *Life of the Marlows*, p. 30.

8. *Ibid.*

9. *Graham Leader*, September 6, 1888.

10. Case No. 235, *United States vs. Alf Marlow et al.*, U.S. Commissioners Court, Graham, Texas, filed September 5, 1888.

11. Case No. 237, *United States vs. Alf Marlow et al.*, U.S. Commissioners Court, Graham, Texas, filed September 5, 1888.

12. Commitment for Alf Marlow et al., U.S. Commissioners Court, Graham, Texas, filed October 10, 1888.

13. Testimony of George Marlow, No. 34, Consolidated, *United States vs. Eugene Logan, Verna Wilkerson and Clint Rutherford*, U.S. District Court, Graham, Texas, October term 1890; *Life of the Marlows*, pp. 31-32.

14. Case No. 234, *United States vs. George Marlow*, U.S. Commissioners Court, Graham, Texas, filed October 8, 1888.

15. *Ibid.*

16. Indictment No 235, *United States vs. Boone Marlow*, U.S. District Court, Graham, Texas, filed October 16, 1888.

17. Indictment No. 236, *United States vs. Epp Marlow*, U.S. District Court, Graham, Texas, filed October 16, 1888.

18. Indictment No. 239, *United States vs. Alf Marlow*, U.S. District Court, Graham, Texas, filed October 16, 1888.

19. Proceedings in U.S. Commissioners Court, Graham, Texas, October 9, 1888.

20. *Ibid.*

21. Appearance Bond of Epp Marlow, No. 236, *United States vs. Epp Marlow*, U.S. Commissioners Court, Graham, Texas, filed October 29, 1888; Appearance Bond of Charles and George Marlow, No. 238, *United States vs. Alf Marlow et al.*, U.S. Commissioners Court, Graham, Texas, filed October 29, 1888; Appearance Bond of Alf Marlow, No. 239, *United States vs. Alf Marlow*, U.S. Commissioners Court, Graham, Texas, filed December 6, 1888.

22. *Life of the Marlows*, pp. 34-35.

23. *Graham Leader*, October 11, 1888.

24. *Ibid.* December 20, 1888; No. 34, Consolidated, *United*

States vs. Eugene Logan, Verna Wilkerson and Clint Rutherford, U.S. District Court, Graham, Texas, October term 1890; "The Historical Saga of the Marlow Brothers," *Montrose* (Colorado) *Daily Press*, March 19, 1988.

Chapter IV

1. Testimony of Charles Marlow, No. 34, Consolidated, *United States vs. Eugene Logan, Verna Wilkerson and Clint Rutherford*, U.S. District Court, Graham, Texas, October term 1890; *Life of the Marlows*, pp. 32-33; *Graham Leader*, December 20, 1888.

2. Testimony of O. G. Denson, No. 34, Consolidated, *United States vs. Eugene Logan, Verna Wilkerson and Clint Rutherford*, U.S. District Court, Graham, Texas, October term 1890; *Life of the Marlows*, p. 61.

3. Testimony of Charles Marlow, No. 34, Consolidated, *United States vs. Eugene Logan, Verna Wilkerson and Clint Rutherford*, U.S. District Court, Graham, Texas, October term 1890.

4. Testimony of John F. Speer and Sam Burns, No. 34, Consolidated, *United States vs. Eugene Logan, Verna Wilkerson and Clint Rutherford*, U.S. District Court, Graham, Texas, October term 1890.

5. Testimony of Charles Marlow and O. G. Denson, No. 34, Consolidated, *United States vs. Eugene Logan, Verna Wilkerson and Clint Rutherford*, U.S. District Court, Graham, Texas, October term 1890.

6. Testimony of George W. Moore, No. 34, Consolidated, *United States vs. Eugene Logan, Verna Wilkerson and Clint Rutherford*, U.S. District Court, Graham, Texas, October term 1890.

7. *Life of the Marlows*, pp. 35-37.

8. Proclamation by the Governor of the State of Texas, L. S. Ross, Austin, Texas, December 19, 1888.

9. *Graham Leader*, December 20 and 27, 1888.

10. Commitment of George Marlow, No. 238; Commitment of Charles Marlow, No. 246; Commitment of Alf Marlow, No. 239; and Commitment of Epp Marlow, No. 238, U.S. Commissioners Court, Graham, Texas, December 24, 1888.

11. Charge of the Court to the Jury by A. P. McCormick, No.

34, Consolidated, *United States vs. Eugene Logan, Verna Wilkerson and Clint Rutherford*, U.S. District Court, Graham, Texas, October term 1890.

12. *Graham Leader*, December 28, 1888.

13. Testimony of Marion Lasater, No. 34, Consolidated, *United States vs. Eugene Logan, Verna Wilkerson and Clint Rutherford*, U.S. District Court, Graham, Texas, October term 1890.

14. Testimony of P. A. Martin, No. 34, Consolidated, *United States vs. Eugene Logan, Verna Wilkerson and Clint Rutherford*, U.S. District Court, Graham, Texas, October term 1890.

15. *Graham Leader*, January 3, 1889.

Chapter V

1. Charge of the Court to the Jury by A. P. McCormick, No. 34, Consolidated, *United States vs. Eugene Logan, Verna Wilkerson and Clint Rutherford*, U.S. District Court, Graham, Texas; *Life of the Marlows*, p. 39.

2. *Life of the Marlows*, 37.

3. Reports of the jail break appear in the *Galveston Daily News*, January 16, 1889, and *Graham Leader*, January 17, 1889.

4. Testimony of Marion Lasater, No. 34, Consolidated, *United States vs. Eugene Logan, Verna Wilkerson and Clint Rutherford*, U.S. District Court, Graham, Texas, October term 1890.

5. Testimony of George Marlow, No. 34, Consolidated, *United States vs. Eugene Logan, Verna Wilkerson and Clint Rutherford*, U.S. District Court, Graham, Texas, October term 1890.

6. Testimony of Marion Lasater, No. 34, Consolidated, *United States vs. Eugene Logan, Verna Wilkerson and Clint Rutherford*, U.S. District Court, Graham, Texas, October term 1890.

7. Testimony of George Marlow, No. 34, Consolidated, *United States vs. Eugene Logan, Verna Wilkerson and Clint Rutherford*, U.S. District Court, Graham, Texas, October term 1890.

8. Testimony of Charles Marlow, No. 34, Consolidated, *United States vs. Eugene Logan, Verna Wilkerson and Clint Rutherford*, U.S. District Court, Graham, Texas, October term 1890.

9. Testimony of A. B. Gant, No. 34, Consolidated, *United States vs. Eugene Logan, Verna Wilkerson and Clint Rutherford*, U.S. District Court, Graham, Texas, October term 1890.

10. Testimony of Bailey Allen, No. 34, Consolidated, *United States vs Eugene Logan, Verna Wilkerson and Clint Rutherford*, U.S. District Court, Graham, Texas, October term 1890.

11. Testimony of Dick Smith and Walter Hamilton, No. 34, Consolidated, *United States vs. Eugene Logan, Verna Wilkerson and Clint Rutherford*, U.S. District Court, Graham, Texas, October term 1890.

12. Testimony of Mrs. R. C. Lauderdale, No. 34, Consolidated, *United States vs. Eugene Logan, Verna Wilkerson and Clint Rutherford*, U.S. District Court, Graham, Texas, October term 1890.

13. Testimony of Marion Lasater, No. 34, Consolidated, *United States vs. Eugene Logan, Verna Wilkerson and Clint Rutherford*, U.S. District Court, Graham, Texas, October term 1890.

14. Testimony of John Taylor and Edwin S. Graham, No. 34, Consolidated, *United States vs. Eugene Logan, Verna Wilkerson and Clint Rutherford*, U.S. District Court, Graham, Texas, October term 1890.

15. Testimony of Mrs. Rickman, No. 34, Consolidated, *United States vs. Eugene Logan, Verna Wilkerson and Clint Rutherford*, U.S. District Court, Graham, Texas, October term 1890.

16. Testimony of Charles and George Marlow, Sam Burns and John Speer, No. 34, Consolidated, *United States vs. Eugene Logan, Verna Wilkerson and Clint Rutherford*, U.S. District Court, Graham, Texas, October term 1890.

17. *Ibid.*

18. *Ibid.*

Chapter VI

1. *Life of the Marlows*, p. 41.

2. Testimony of P. A. Martin, No. 34, Consolidated, *United States vs. Eugene Logan, Verna Wilkerson and Clint Rutherford*, U.S. District Court, Graham, Texas, October term 1890.

3. Testimony of T. A. Gay, No. 34, Consolidated, *United States vs. Eugene Logan, Verna Wilkerson and Clint Rutherford*, U.S. District Court, Graham, Texas, October term 1890.

4. Testimony of P. A. Martin, No. 34, Consolidated, *United States vs. Eugene Logan, Verna Wilkerson and Clint Rutherford*, U.S. District Court, Graham, Texas, October term 1890.

5. Testimony of John Putman, No. 34, Consolidated, *United States vs. Eugene Logan, Verna Wilkerson and Clint Rutherford*, U.S. District Court, Graham, Texas, October term 1890.

6. Testimony of Mrs. Vance, No. 34, Consolidated, *United States vs. Eugene Logan, Verna Wilkerson and Clint Rutherford*, U.S. District Court, Graham, Texas, October term 1890.

7. Testimony of John Speer, No. 34, Consolidated, *United States vs. Eugene Logan, Verna Wilkerson and Clint Rutherford*, U.S. District Court, Graham, Texas, October term 1890.

8. Testimony of John Taylor, No. 34, Consolidated, *United States vs. Eugene Logan, Verna Wilkerson and Clint Rutherford*, U.S. District Court, Graham, Texas, October term 1890.

9. *Ibid.*

10. Testimony of Marion Lasater, No. 34, Consolidated, *United States vs. Eugene Logan, Verna Wilkerson and Clint Rutherford*, U.S. District Court, Graham, Texas, October term 1890.

11. Testimony of P. A. Martin, No. 34, Consolidated, *United States vs. Eugene Logan, Verna Wilkerson and Clint Rutherford*, U.S. District Court, Graham, Texas, October term 1890.

12. Testimony of J. T. Lovejoy, No. 34, Consolidated, *United States vs. Eugene Logan, Verna Wilkerson and Clint Rutherford*, U.S. District Court, Graham, Texas, October term 1890.

13. Testimony of Charles Marlow, No. 34, Consolidated, *United States vs. Eugene Logan, Verna Wilkerson and Clint Rutherford*, U.S. District Court, Graham, Texas, October term 1890.

14. Testimony of P. A. Martin, No. 34, Consolidated, *United States vs. Eugene Logan, Verna Wilkerson and Clint Rutherford*, U.S. District Court, Graham, Texas, October term 1890.

15. Testimony of Charles Marlow, No. 34, Consolidated, *United States vs. Eugene Logan, Verna Wilkerson and Clint Rutherford*, U.S. District Court, Graham, Texas, October term 1980.

Chapter VII

1. Details of the battle, conversation quotes, and escape of the Marlows from Dry Creek appear in the *Galveston Daily News*, January 21, 1889, and *Graham Leader*, January 24, 1889. Also, testimony of George and Charles Marlow, No. 34, Consolidated, *United States vs. Eugene Logan, Verna Wilkerson and Clint*

Rutherford, U.S. District Court, Graham, Texas, October term 1890.

2. Testimony of George Marlow, No. 34, Consolidated, *United States vs. Eugene Logan, Verna Wilkerson and Clint Rutherford*, U.S. District Court, Graham, Texas, October term 1890.

Chapter VIII

1. Testimony of Joe and Lizzie White, No. 34, Consolidated, *United States vs. Eugene Logan, Verna Wilkerson and Clint Rutherford*, U.S. District Court, Graham, Texas, October term 1890.

2. Testimony of Marion Lasater, No. 34, Consolidated, *United States vs. Eugene Logan, Verna Wilkerson and Clint Rutherford*, U.S. District Court, Graham, Texas, October term 1890.

3. Testimony of Perry Harmison, No. 34, Consolidated, *United States vs. Eugene Logan, Verna Wilkerson and Clint Rutherford*, U.S. District Court, Graham, Texas, October term 1890.

4. Testimony of George W. Moore, No. 34, Consolidated, *United States vs. Eugene Logan, Verna Wilkerson and Clint Rutherford*, U.S. District Court, Graham, Texas, October term 1890.

5. *Ibid.*

6. *Life of the Marlows*, p. 53.

7. Testimony of George W. Moore, No. 34, Consolidated, *United States vs. Eugene Logan, Verna Wilkerson and Clint Rutherford*, U.S. District Court, Graham, Texas, October term 1890.

8. Testimony of Charley Auburg, No. 34, Consolidated, *United States vs. Eugene Logan, Verna Wilkerson and Clint Rutherford*, U.S. District Court, Graham, Texas, October term 1890.

9. Testimony of Marion Lasater, No. 34, Consolidated, *United States vs. Eugene Logan, Verna Wilkerson and Clint Rutherford*, U.S. District Court, Graham, Texas, October term 1890.

10. Testimony of George Marlow, No. 34, Consolidated, *United States vs. Eugene Logan, Verna Wilkerson and Clint Rutherford*, U.S. District Court, Graham, Texas, October term 1890; *Life of the Marlows*, p. 54.

11. Testimony of W. F. Morton, No. 34, Consolidated, *United*

States vs. Eugene Logan, Verna Wilkerson and Clint Rutherford, U.S. District Court, Graham, Texas, October term 1890.

12. Testimony of Charley Auburg, No. 34, Consolidated, *United States vs. Eugene Logan, Verna Wilkerson and Clint Rutherford*, U.S. District Court, Graham, Texas, October term 1890.

13. Testimony of W. F. Morton, No. 34, Consolidated, *United States vs. Eugene Logan, Verna Wilkerson and Clint Rutherford*, U.S. District Court, Graham, Texas, October term 1890.

14. *Ibid.*

15. *Galveston Daily News*, January 25, 1889.

16. *Ibid.* (dispatch from Dallas) January 29, 1889; *Graham Leader*, January 31, 1889.

17. *Life of the Marlows*, pp. 55-56, 58; testimony of P. A. Martin as to inquest proceedings over body of Boone Marlow, No. 34, Consolidated, *United States vs. Eugene Logan, Verna Wilkerson and Clint Rutherford*, U.S. District Court, Graham, Texas, October term 1890.

18. *Graham Leader*, March 28, 1889.

19. *Graham Leader*, October 29, 1889; Crouch, *A History of Young County, Texas*, p. 118.

20. *Life of the Marlows*, p. 57.

Chapter IX

1. Testimony of A. B. Gant, No. 34, Consolidated, *United States vs. Eugene Logan, Verna Wilkerson and Clint Rutherford*, U.S. District Court, Graham, Texas, October term 1890.

2. Testimony of Dixie Criswell, No. 34, Consolidated, *United States vs. Eugene Logan, Verna Wilkerson and Clint Rutherford*, U.S. District Court, Graham, Texas, October term 1890.

3. Testimony of Mrs. R.C. Lauderdale, No. 34, Consolidated, *United States vs. Eugene Logan, Verna Wilkerson and Clint Rutherford*, U.S. District Court, Graham, Texas, October term 1890.

4. Testimony of P. A. Martin, No. 34, Consolidated, *United States vs. Eugene Logan, Verna Wilkerson and Clint Rutherford*, U.S. District Court, Graham, Texas, October term 1890.

5. Testimony of O. G. Denson, No. 34, Consolidated, *United States vs. Eugene Logan, Verna Wilkerson and Clint Rutherford*, U.S. District Court, Graham, Texas, October term 1890.

6. Testimony of Broiles and Kramer, No. 34, Consolidated, *United*

States vs. Eugene Logan, Verna Wilkerson and Clint Rutherford, U.S. District Court, Graham, Texas, October term 1890.

7. Testimony of James Duty, No. 34, Consolidated, *United States vs. Eugene Logan, Verna Wilkerson and Clint Rutherford*, U.S. District Court, Graham, Texas, October term 1890.

8. *Ibid.*

9 Testimony of Les Randolph, No. 34, Consolidated, *United States vs. Eugene Logan, Verna Wilkerson and Clint Rutherford*, U.S. District Court, Graham, Texas, October term 1890.

10. Testimony of W.F. Morton, No. 34, Consolidated, *United States vs. Eugene Logan, Verna Wilkerson and Clint Rutherford*, U.S. District Court, Graham, Texas, October term 1890.

11. Indictment No. 456, *United States vs. Eugene Logan et al.*, Conspiracy to Obstruct and Resist U.S. Deputy Marshal in Executing Writs of Commitments, U.S. District and Circuit Court, Dallas, Texas, filed February 6, 1889.

12. *Graham Leader*, January 31, 1889.

13. *Ibid.*, March 14, 1889.

14. *Ibid.*

15. *Ibid.*, March 28, 1889.

16. *Life of the Marlows*, p. 57.

17. *Graham Leader*, March 18, 1889.

18. *Life of the Marlows*, p. 89.

19. *Ibid.*

Chapter X

1. *Graham Leader*, April 25, 1889.

2. *Ibid.*, August 15, 1889.

3. *Ibid.*, August 8 and 22, 1889.

4. *Life of the Marlows*, p. 59.

5. *Graham Leader*, November 28, 1889.

6. *Ibid.*

7. *Ibid.*, December 5, 1889.

Chapter XI

1. Application of Sam Waggoner and William Williams for Witnesses, *ex parte Eugene Logan et al.*, filed February 21, 1890.

2. Defendants' Motion to Quash Indictments, *United States vs. Eugene Logan et al.*, filed February 25, 1890.

3. Application of Defendants for Bail, *United States vs. Eugene Logan et al.*, filed February 27, 1890.

4. Attachment for George Marlow, filed March 20, 1890; Attachment for Charles Marlow, filed March 21, 1890, *United States vs. Eugene Logan et al.*

5. *Life of the Marlows*, p. 90.

6. *Ibid.*, pp. 90-91.

7. *Ibid.*, p. 91.

8. Motion to Consolidate, No. 34, *United States vs. Eugene Logan et al.*, filed October 21, 1890.

9. Defendants' Motion to Quash Indictment No. 34, *United States vs. Eugene Logan et al.*, filed October 22, 1890.

10. Order for Special Venire, No. 34, Consolidated, *United States vs. Eugene Logan et al.*, filed October 22, 1890.

11. Motion to Quash Special Venire, No. 34, Consolidated, *United States vs. Eugene Logan et al.*, filed October 30, 1890.

12. Application for Witnesses, No. 34, Consolidated, *United States vs. Eugene Logan, Verna Wilkerson and Clint Rutherford*, filed November 5, 1890.

Chapter XII

1. *Life of the Marlows*, p. 60.

2. *Graham Leader*, November 12 and 19, 1890.

3. Testimony of P. A. Martin, No. 34, Consolidated, *United States vs. Eugene Logan, Verna Wilkerson and Clint Rutherford*, trial of November 1890.

4. Verdict and Commitment, No. 34, Consolidated, *United States vs. Eugene Logan, Verna Wilkerson and Clint Rutherford*, trial of November 1890.

5. *Graham Leader*, December 10, 1890.

6. *Life of the Marlows*, p. 73.

Chapter XIII

1. *Graham Leader*, March 11, 1890.

2. *Ibid.*

170

3. Motion to Quash Indictment by John Levell et al., No. 34, Consolidated, *United States vs. Eugene Logan et al.*, filed March 16, 1891.

4. Special Plea of Former Jeopardy by Eugene Logan and Verna Wilkerson, No. 34, Consolidated, *United States vs. Eugene Logan et al.*, filed March 16, 1891.

5. Application for Order to Sever No. 34, Consolidated, *United States vs. Eugene Logan et al.*, filed March 16, 1891.

6. Motion for Service of Special Venire List of Government Witnesses, No. 34, Consolidated, *United States vs. Eugene Logan et al.*, filed March 26, 1891.

7. *Graham Leader*, April 1, 1891.

8. Trial proceedings, No. 34, Consolidated, *United States vs. Eugene Logan et al.*

9. *Graham Leader*, April 1, 1891.

10. Trial proceedings, No. 34, Consolidated, *United States vs. Eugene Logan, et al.*

11. *Ibid.*

12. *Ibid.*

13. Charge of the Court to the Jury, No. 34, Consolidated, *United States vs. Eugene Logan et al.*, April 14, 1891.

14. Verdict of the Jury, No. 34, Consolidated, *United States vs. Eugene Logan et al.*, filed April 17, 1891.

15. *Graham Leader*, April 22, 1891.

16. Defendants' Special Charges Requested, No. 34, Consolidated, *United States vs. Eugene Logan et al.*, filed April 17, 1891.

17. Commitments for Eugene Logan, Sam Waggoner and Marion Wallace, No. 34 Consolidated, *United States vs. Eugene Logan et al.*, filed April 18, 1891.

Chapter XIV

1. Defendants' Bill of Exceptions, 1-33, and Defendants' Petition for Writ of Error, No. 34, Consolidated, *United States vs. Eugene Logan et al.*, filed April 18, 1891.

2. Petition for Habeas Corpus, No. 34, Consolidated, *United States vs. Eugene Logan et al.*, filed May 22, 1891.

3. No. 1235, Supreme Court of the United States, *Eugene Logan et al., Plaintiffs in Error vs. United States*, August 1, 1891.

171

4. Bond of Sam Waggoner, No. 34, Consolidated, *United States vs. Eugene Logan et al.*, filed September 8, 1891.

5. *Life of the Marlows*, pp. 81-82.

6. *Ibid.*, pp. 82-83.

7. *Ibid.*, p. 83

Chapter XV

1. Vol. 12, *Supreme Court Reporter*, p. 617.

2. Mandate, No. 1235, Supreme Court of the United States, *Eugene Logan et al., Plaintiffs in Error vs. United States*, April 14, 1892, filed May 30, 1892.

Chapter XVI

1. *Life of the Marlows*, pp. 74-75.

2. *Ibid.*

3. Crouch, *A History of Young County, Texas*, p. 121.

4. *Graham Leader*, February 4, 1891.

5. *Ibid.*

6. Crouch, *A History of Young County, Texas*, p. 122.

7. *Ibid.*, p. 121.

8. *Life of the Marlows*, pp. 95-96.

9. *Ibid.*, p. 94.

10. *Ibid.*, p. 92-95.

11. Josephine Patten, "He Killed A Heap of Men," *Old West*, vol. 3, no. 2, Winter 1966.

12. *Life of the Marlows*, p. 99.

13. *Ibid.*

14. Patten, "He Killed A Heap of Men."

Bibliography

Manuscripts and Documents

Certificate of Death of Charles Marlow, January 19, 1941 (County Registrar Recorder, Los Angeles County, Department of Public Health, State of California).

Certificate of Death of George Marlow, July 3, 1945 (Local Register, Montrose County, Bureau of Vital Statistics, State of Colorado).

Commission of George Marlow as Special Deputy U.S. Marshal, Dallas, Texas, January 29, 1891 (see *Life of the Marlows*).

Commission of Charles Marlow as Special Deputy U.S. Marshal, Dallas, Texas, January 29, 1891 (See *Life of the Marlows*).

Correspondence and telephone communications of author with Marlow descendants (1989-1991).

Proclamation by the Governor of the State of Texas, L. S. Ross (reward for Boone Marlow), Austin, Texas, December 19, 1888.

Records of the United States Circuit and District Courts and the U.S. Commissioners Courts of the Northern District of Texas

[Unless otherwise indicated, manuscripts and records dealing with the Northern District Court at Graham, Texas, can be found at the National Archives and Records Administration, Federal Records Center, Fort Worth, Texas.]

August 18, 1888, Case no. 238, *United States vs. Alf Marlow et al.*, U.S. Commissioners Court, Graham, Texas.

September 5, 1888, Case no. 235, *United States vs. Alf Marlow et al.*, U.S. Commissioners Court, Graham, Texas.

September 5, 1888, Case no. 237, *United States vs. Alf Marlow et al.*, U.S. Commissioners Court, Graham, Texas.

October 8, 1888, Case no. 234, *United States vs. George Marlow*, U.S. Commissioners Court, Graham, Texas.

October 8, 1888, Warrant, Case no. 234, *United States vs. George Marlow*, U.S. Commissioners Court, Graham, Texas.

October 9, 1888, Proceedings in U.S. Commissioners Court, Graham, Texas.

October 10, 1888, Commitment for Alf Marlow et al., U.S. Commissioners Court, Graham, Texas.

October 16, 1888, Indictment no. 235, *United States vs. Boone Marlow*, U.S. District Court, Graham, Texas.

October 16, 1888, Indictment no. 236, *United States vs. Epp Marlow*, U.S. District Court, Graham, Texas.

October 16, 1888, Indictment no. 239, *United States vs. Alf Marlow*, U.S. District Court, Graham, Texas.

October 29, 1888, Apearance Bond of Epp Marlow, no. 236, *United States vs. Epp Marlow*, U.S. Commissioners Court, Graham, Texas.

October 29, 1888, Appearance Bond of Charles and George Marlow, no. 238, *United States vs. Alf Marlow et al.*, U.S. Commissioners Court, Graham, Texas.

December 6, 1888, Appearance Bond of Alf Marlow, no. 239, *United States vs. Alf Marlow*, U.S. Commissioners Court, Graham, Texas.

December 24, 1888, no. 238, Commitment for Alf Marlow, *United States vs. Alf Marlow et al.*, U.S. Commissioners Court, Graham, Texas.

December 24, 1888, no. 238, Commitment for George Marlow, *United States vs. Alf Marlow et al.*, U.S. Commissioners Court, Graham, Texas.

December 24, 1888, no. 238, Commitment for Epp Marlow, *United States vs. Alf Marlow et al.*, U.S. Commissioners Court, Graham, Texas.

December 27, 1888, no. 246, Commitment for Charles Marlow, *United States vs. Charles Marlow*, U.S. Commissioners Court, Graham, Texas.

December 29, 1888, no. 241, Warrant, *United States vs. Boone Marlow*, U.S. Commissioners Court, Graham, Texas.

February 6, 1889, Indictment no. 456, U.S. District and Circuit Court for Northern District of Texas, Dallas, January 26, 1889: transferred for prosecution to U.S. District Court, Graham, as Case no. 263, *United States vs. Eugene Logan et al.*

February 11, 1890, Indictment no. 492, U.S. District and Circuit Court for Northern District of Texas, Dallas; transferred for prosecution to U.S. District Court, Graham, as Case no. 33, *United States vs. Eugene Logan.*

February 11, 1890, Indictment no. 493, U.S. District and Circuit Court for Northern District of Texas, Dallas; transferred for prosecution to U.S. District Court, Graham, as case no. 34, *United States vs. Eugene Logan et al.*

February 11, 1890, Indictment no. 494, U.S. District and Circuit Court for Northern District of Texas, Dallas; transferred for prosecution to U.S. District Court, Graham, as Case no. 36, *United States vs. Eugene Logan et al.*

February 21, 1890, Application of Sam Waggoner and William Williams for Witnesses, *Ex parte Eugene Logan et al.*

February 25, 1890, Defendants' Motion to Quash Indictments, *United States vs. Eugene Logan et al.*

February 27, 1890, Application of Defendants for Bail, *United States vs. Eugene Logan et al.*

March 20, 1890, Attachment for George Marlow as Competent Witness, *United States vs. Eugene Logan et al.*

March 21, 1890, Attachment for Charles Marlow as competent Witness, *United States vs. Eugene Logan et al.*

October 21, 1890, Motion to Consolidate Cases 33, 34, 35, and 36 as no. 34, Consolidated, *United States vs. Eugene Logan et al.*

October 22, 1890, Order for Special Venire, no. 34, Consolidated, *United States vs. Eugene Logan et al.*

October 22, 1890, Defendants' Motion to Quash Indictment no. 34, Consolidated, *United States vs. Eugene Logan et al.*

October 30, 1890, Defendants' Motion to Quash Special Venire, no. 34, Consolidated, *United States vs. Eugene Logan et al.*

November 5, 1890, Defendants' Application for Witnesses, no. 34, Consolidated, *United States vs. Eugene Logan, Verna Wilkerson and Clint Rutherford.*

November 6-21, 1890, Testimony in no. 34, Consolidated, *United States vs. Eugene Logan, Verna Wilkerson and Clint Rutherford*, U.S. District Court, Graham, Texas, October term 1890.

November 22, 1890, Verdict and Commitment, no. 34, Consolidated, *United States vs. Eugene Logan, Verna Wilkerson and Clint Rutherford*.

March 16, 1891, Motion to Quash Indictment by John Levell et al., no. 34, Consolidated, *United States vs. Eugene Logan et al.*

March 16, 1891, Special Plea of Former Jeopardy by Eugene Logan and Verna Wilkerson, no. 34, Consolidated, *United States vs. Eugene Logan et al.*

March 16, 1891, Application for Order to Sever, no. 34, Consolidated, *United States vs. Eugene Logan et al.*

March 26, 1891, Motion for Service of Special Venire List of Government Witnesses, *United States vs. Eugene Logan et al.*

April 14, 1891, Charge of the Court to the Jury, no. 34, Consolidated, *United States vs. Eugene Logan et al.*

April 17, 1891, Verdict of Jury, no. 34, Consolidated, *United States vs. Eugene Logan et al.*

April 17, 1891, Defendants' Motion for New Trial, no. 34, Consolidated, *United States vs. Eugene Logan et al.*

April 18, 1891, Commitments for Eugene Logan, Sam Waggoner and Marion Wallace, no. 34, Consolidated, *United States vs. Eugene Logan et al.*

April 18, 1891, Defendants' Bill of Exceptions, no. 34, Consolidated, *United States vs. Eugene Logan et al.*

April 18, 1891, Defendants' Petition for Writ of Error, no. 34, Consolidated, *United States vs. Eugene Logan et al.*

May 22, 1891, Petition for Habeas Corpus, no. 34, Consolidated, *United States vs. Eugene Logan et al.*

May 29, 1891, Defendants' Assignment of Errors, no. 34, Consolidated, *United States vs. Eugene Logan et al*

August 1, 1891, Order for Bail, no. 1235, Supreme Court of the United States, *Eugene Logan et al., Plaintiffs in Error vs. United States.*

September 8, 1891, Bond of Sam Waggoner, no. 34, Consolidated, *United States vs. Eugene Logan et al.*

October term 1891, Supreme Court of the United States, *Eugene Logan et al., Plaintiffs in Error vs. United States.*

April 4, 1892, Mandate, no. 1235, Supreme Court of the United

States, *Eugene Logan et al., Plaintiffs in Error vs. United States,* no. 34, Consolidated, *United States vs. Eugene Logan et al.,* reversed and remanded for trial.

Tax Lists and Assessments Rolls, Ouray County, Colorado, 1891-1920.

Newspapers

Dallas Morning News, October, November, December 1889; July 1890; January 1891.

Fort Worth Evening Mail, November 1889.

Fort Worth Gazette, November 1889.

Galveston Daily News, December 1888; January, February, March, April 1889.

Graham Leader, September, October 1886; September, December 1888; January, February, March, April, May, August, October, November, December 1889; October, November, December 1890; February, March, April 1891.

Montrose (Colorado) *Daily Press,* October 1907; June 1916; September 1918; June 1933; October 1936; January 1941; July 1945; March 1988.

Muskogee (Oklahoma) *Phoenix,* September 1888.

Weatherford (Texas) *Sun,* October, November 1889.

Books and Pamphlets

Barrett, Thomas. *The Great Hanging at Gainesville, Cooke County, Texas, October A.D. 1862* (Gainesville, Texas: Privately printed, January 1885, Reprinted by Texas State Historical Association, Austin, 1961).

Brown, Robert L. *An Empire of Silver, a History of the San Juan Silver Rush* (Caldwell, Idaho: The Caxton Printers, Ltd., 1965).

Cotner, Robert C. *James Stephen Hogg, A Biography* (Austin: University of Texas Press, 1959).

Crouch, Carrie J. *A History of Young County, Texas* (Austin: Texas State Historical Association, 1956).

Davis, William C. (ed.) *The Confederate General* (n.p.: A Publication of the National Historical Society, 1991), vol. 1.

Halsell, H. H. *Cowboys and Cattleland* (Nashville, Tennessee: The

Parthenon Press, 1937, Reprinted by Texas Christian University Press, 1983).

Hendricks, George David. *The Bad Man of the West* (San Antonio: The Naylor Company, 1941).

Hill, Luther B. *A History of the State of Oklahoma* (Chicago and New York: The Lewis Publishing Company, 1908), vol. 1.

Holloway, Carroll C. *Texas Gun Lore* (San Antonio: The Naylor Company, 1951).

Jessen, Kenneth. *Colorado Gunsmoke, True Stories of Outlaws and Lawmen on the Colorado Frontier* (Boulder, Colorado: Pruett Publishing Company, 1986).

Ledbetter, Barbara A. Neal. *Fort Belknap, Frontier Saga* (Burnet, Texas: Eakin Press, 1982).

Marlow, Charles and George Marlow. *Life of the Marlows, A True Story of Frontier Life in the Early Days.* As Related by Themselves. (Ouray, Colorado: Plaindealer Print, Kelly & Hulaniski, Publishers, 1892; Revised by William Rathmell, Ouray Herald Print, W. S. Olexa, Publisher, 1928).

Mason, Tyler. *Riding for Texas: The True Adventures of Captain Bill McDonald of the Texas Rangers* (New York: Reynal and Hitchock, A John Day Book, 1936).

Morgan, E. Buford. *The Wichita Mountains, Ancient Oasis of the Prairie* (Waco, Texas: Texian Press, 1973).

Oklahoma, A Guide to the Sooner State. Compiled by the Writers' Program of the Works Projects Administration. American Guide Series (Norman: University of Oklahoma Press, 1941).

Ragland, Hobert D. *A History of Rush Springs* (Rush Springs, Oklahoma: Gazette Publishing Company, 1952).

Raine, William MacLeod. *Famous Sheriffs and Western Outlaws* (Garden City, New York: Doubleday, Doran and Company, Inc., 1929).

Raine, William MacLeod and Will C. Barnes. *Cattle* (Garden City, New York: Doubleday, Doran and Company, Inc., 1930).

Rockwell, Wilson (ed.). *Memoirs of A Lawman* (Denver: Sage Books, 1962).

Rogers, John William. *The Lusty Texans of Dallas* (New York: E.P. Dutton and Company, Inc., 1951).

Shirley, Glenn. *Toughest of Them All* (Albuquerque: University of New Mexico Press, 1953).

Siringo, Charles A. *Riata and Spurs, The Story of a Lifetime Spent in the Saddle as Cowboy and Ranger* (Boston: Houghton Mifflin Company, 1937).

Sonnichsen, C. L. *I'll Die Before I'll Run, The Story of the Great Feuds of Texas* (New York: Harper and Brothers, Publishers, 1951).

Speer, William S. and John Henry Brown (eds.). *The Encyclopedia of the New West* (Marshall, Texas: The United States Biographical Publishing Company, 1881).

Stone, Wilbur Fisk (ed.). *History of Colorado* (Chicago: The S. J. Clarke Publishing Company, 1918), vol. 1.

Taylor, Ralph C. *Colorado South of the Border* (Denver, Colorado: Sage Books, 1963).

Thoburn, Joseph B. *A Standard History of Oklahoma* (Chicago and New York: The American Historical Society, 1916), vols. 1, 2

Wilson, Torrence. "A History of Wilbarger County, Texas" (M.A. thesis, University of Texas, Austin, 1938).

Articles

Capps, Mary Neely. "The Navajo Peaks." *Oklahoma Today*, vol. 27, no. 2, Spring 1977.

Christian, Bill. "The Marlows: Famous or Infamous?" *Orbit Magazine, Daily Oklahoman*, March 4, 1973.

"County Named for Colonel Wm. Young." *Graham News*, August 24, 1967.

Dale, Edward Everett. "Old Navajoe." *Chronicles of Oklahoma*, vol. 26, no. 2, Summer 1946.

"Historical Notes." *Chronicles of Oklahoma*, vol. 20, no. 2, June 1942.

"Historical Notes and Comments." *Chronicles of Oklahoma*, vol. 20, no. 3, September 1942.

"The Historical Saga of the Marlow Brothers." *Montrose* (Colorado) *Daily Press*, March 10, 1988.

"Hunted in the Law's Name: Four Men in Shackles Against A Hundred, Border Life in Texas, The Famous Marlow Mob Case." *National Police Gazette*, June 1891.

Johnson, Edward M. "Deputy Marshal Johnson Breaks A Long Silence." *True West*, vol. 27, no. 3, January-February 1980.

"Marlow, a Rapidly Growing City With a Most Brilliant Future."
Daily Oklahoman, June 3, 1903.

"Outstanding Jurist Held First Federal Court." *Graham News*, May
5, 1974.

Patten, Josephine, "He Killed A Heap of Men." *Old West*, vol. 1,
no. 3, Winter 1966.

Raine, William MacLeod. "Texas as Was." *Frontier Stories*, vol. 7,
no. 4, January 1928. (Reprinted in *Famous Sheriffs and Western
Outlaws*).

"The Fighting Marlows." *Empire Magazine, The Denver Post*, June
21, 1963.

"Remarkable History of the Marlow Family." *Montrose* (Colorado)
Daily Press, October 18, 1907.

Shirley, Glenn. "Hell Riders of the Brazos." *Western Aces*, vol. 18,
no. 4, April 1943. (Reprinted as "Buckshot on the Brazos" in
Toughest of Them All).

Rayburn, Dal. "We Come to Get You, Boone Marlow." *Men, True
Adventure*, vol. 7, no. 12, December 1958.

Stanley, Samuel. "A Desperate Escape." *Real West*, vol. 29, no. 211,
December 1986.

Taylor, Nat M. "Story of the Marlow Boys." *True West*, vol. 9, no.
3, January-February 1962.

Index

181